OECD/G20 Base Erosion and Profit Shifting Project

Preventing the Granting of Treaty Benefits in Inappropriate Circumstances, Action 6 - 2015 Final Report

OECD
BETTER POLICIES FOR BETTER LIVES

This document and any map included herein are without prejudice to the status of or sovereignty over any territory, to the delimitation of international frontiers and boundaries and to the name of any territory, city or area.

Please cite this publication as:
OECD (2015), *Preventing the Granting of Treaty Benefits in Inappropriate Circumstances, Action 6 - 2015 Final Report*, OECD/G20 Base Erosion and Profit Shifting Project, OECD Publishing, Paris.
http://dx.doi.org/10.1787/9789264241695-en

ISBN 978-92-64-24120-6 (print)
ISBN 978-92-64-24169-5 (PDF)

Series: OECD/G20 Base Erosion and Profit Shifting Project
ISSN 2313-2604 (print)
ISSN 2313-2612 (online)

Photo credits: Cover © ninog – Fotolia.com

Corrigenda to OECD publications may be found on line at: *www.oecd.org/about/publishing/corrigenda.htm*.

Foreword

International tax issues have never been as high on the political agenda as they are today. The integration of national economies and markets has increased substantially in recent years, putting a strain on the international tax rules, which were designed more than a century ago. Weaknesses in the current rules create opportunities for base erosion and profit shifting (BEPS), requiring bold moves by policy makers to restore confidence in the system and ensure that profits are taxed where economic activities take place and value is created.

Following the release of the report *Addressing Base Erosion and Profit Shifting* in February 2013, OECD and G20 countries adopted a 15-point Action Plan to address BEPS in September 2013. The Action Plan identified 15 actions along three key pillars: introducing coherence in the domestic rules that affect cross-border activities, reinforcing substance requirements in the existing international standards, and improving transparency as well as certainty.

Since then, all G20 and OECD countries have worked on an equal footing and the European Commission also provided its views throughout the BEPS project. Developing countries have been engaged extensively via a number of different mechanisms, including direct participation in the Committee on Fiscal Affairs. In addition, regional tax organisations such as the African Tax Administration Forum, the *Centre de rencontre des administrations fiscales* and the *Centro Interamericano de Administraciones Tributarias*, joined international organisations such as the International Monetary Fund, the World Bank and the United Nations, in contributing to the work. Stakeholders have been consulted at length: in total, the BEPS project received more than 1 400 submissions from industry, advisers, NGOs and academics. Fourteen public consultations were held, streamed live on line, as were webcasts where the OECD Secretariat periodically updated the public and answered questions.

After two years of work, the 15 actions have now been completed. All the different outputs, including those delivered in an interim form in 2014, have been consolidated into a comprehensive package. The BEPS package of measures represents the first substantial renovation of the international tax rules in almost a century. Once the new measures become applicable, it is expected that profits will be reported where the economic activities that generate them are carried out and where value is created. BEPS planning strategies that rely on outdated rules or on poorly co-ordinated domestic measures will be rendered ineffective.

Implementation therefore becomes key at this stage. The BEPS package is designed to be implemented via changes in domestic law and practices, and via treaty provisions, with negotiations for a multilateral instrument under way and expected to be finalised in 2016. OECD and G20 countries have also agreed to continue to work together to ensure a consistent and co-ordinated implementation of the BEPS recommendations. Globalisation requires that global solutions and a global dialogue be established which go beyond OECD and G20 countries. To further this objective, in 2016 OECD and G20 countries will conceive an inclusive framework for monitoring, with all interested countries participating on an equal footing.

A better understanding of how the BEPS recommendations are implemented in practice could reduce misunderstandings and disputes between governments. Greater focus on implementation and tax administration should therefore be mutually beneficial to governments and business. Proposed improvements to data and analysis will help support ongoing evaluation of the quantitative impact of BEPS, as well as evaluating the impact of the countermeasures developed under the BEPS Project.

Table of contents

Abbreviations and acronyms . . . 7

Executive summary . . . 9

Introduction . . . 13

A. Treaty provisions and/or domestic rules to prevent the granting of treaty benefits in inappropriate circumstances . . . 17
  1. Cases where a person tries to circumvent limitations provided by the treaty itself . . . 17
    a) Treaty shopping . . . 17
      i) Limitation-on-benefits rule . . . 20
      ii) Rules aimed at arrangements one of the principal purposes of which is to obtain treaty benefits . . . 54
    b) Other situations where a person seeks to circumvent treaty limitations . . . 69
      i) Splitting-up of contracts . . . 69
      ii) Hiring-out of labour cases . . . 69
      iii) Transactions intended to avoid dividend characterisation . . . 69
      iv) Dividend transfer transactions . . . 70
      v) Transactions that circumvent the application of Article 13(4) . . . 71
      vi) Tie-breaker rule for determining the treaty residence of dual-resident persons other than individuals . . . 72
      vii) Anti-abuse rule for permanent establishments situated in third States . . . 75
  2. Cases where a person tries to abuse the provisions of domestic tax law using treaty benefits . . . 78
    a) Application of tax treaties to restrict a Contracting State's right to tax its own residents . . . 86
    b) Departure or exit taxes . . . 89
B. Clarification that tax treaties are not intended to be used to generate double non-taxation . . . 91
C. Tax policy considerations that, in general, countries should consider before deciding to enter into a tax treaty with another country . . . 94

Bibliography . . . 101

Abbreviations and acronyms

BEPS	Base erosion and profit shifting
CIV	Collective investment vehicles
LOB	Limitation-on-benefits
OECD	Organisation for Economic Co-operation and Development
PPT	Principal purposes test
REIT	Real Estate Investment Trust
RIC	Regulated Investment Company
VCLT	Vienna Convention on the Law of Treaties

Executive summary

Action 6 of the OECD/G20 Base Erosion and Profit Shifting (BEPS) Project identifies treaty abuse, and in particular treaty shopping, as one of the most important sources of BEPS concerns.

Taxpayers engaged in treaty shopping and other treaty abuse strategies undermine tax sovereignty by claiming treaty benefits in situations where these benefits were not intended to be granted, thereby depriving countries of tax revenues. Countries have therefore agreed to include anti-abuse provisions in their tax treaties, including a minimum standard to counter treaty shopping. They also agree that some flexibility in the implementation of the minimum standard is required as these provisions need to be adapted to each country's specificities and to the circumstances of the negotiation of bilateral conventions.

Section A of this report includes new treaty anti-abuse rules that provide safeguards against the abuse of treaty provisions and offer a certain degree of flexibility regarding how to do so.

These new treaty anti-abuse rules first address treaty shopping, which involves strategies through which a person who is not a resident of a State attempts to obtain benefits that a tax treaty concluded by that State grants to residents of that State, for example by establishing a letterbox company in that State. The following approach is recommended to deal with these strategies:

- First, a clear statement that the States that enter into a tax treaty intend to avoid creating opportunities for non-taxation or reduced taxation through tax evasion or avoidance, including through treaty shopping arrangements will be included in tax treaties (this recommendation is included in Section B of the report).
- Second, a specific anti-abuse rule, the limitation-on-benefits (LOB) rule, that limits the availability of treaty benefits to entities that meet certain conditions will be included in the OECD Model Tax Convention. These conditions, which are based on the legal nature, ownership in, and general activities of the entity, seek to ensure that there is a sufficient link between the entity and its State of residence. Such limitation-on-benefits provisions are currently found in treaties concluded by a few countries and have proven to be effective in preventing many forms of treaty shopping strategies.
- Third, in order to address other forms of treaty abuse, including treaty shopping situations that would not be covered by the LOB rule described above, a more general anti-abuse rule based on the principal purposes of transactions or arrangements (the principal purposes test or "PPT" rule) will be included in the OECD Model Tax Convention. Under that rule, if one of the principal purposes of transactions or arrangements is to obtain treaty benefits, these benefits would be denied unless it is established that granting these benefits would be in accordance with the object and purpose of the provisions of the treaty.

The report recognises that each of the LOB and PPT rules has strengths and weaknesses and may not be appropriate for, or accord with the treaty policy of, all countries. Also, the domestic law of some countries may include provisions that make it unnecessary to combine these two rules to prevent treaty shopping.

Given the risk to revenues posed by treaty shopping, countries have committed to ensure a minimum level of protection against treaty shopping (the "minimum standard"). That commitment will require countries to include in their tax treaties an express statement that their common intention is to eliminate double taxation without creating opportunities for non-taxation or reduced taxation through tax evasion or avoidance, including through treaty shopping arrangements. Countries will implement this common intention by including in their treaties: (i) the combined approach of an LOB and PPT rule described above, (ii) the PPT rule alone, or (iii) the LOB rule supplemented by a mechanism that would deal with conduit financing arrangements not already dealt with in tax treaties.

Section A also includes new rules to be included in tax treaties in order to address other forms of treaty abuse. These targeted rules address (1) certain dividend transfer transactions that are intended to lower artificially withholding taxes payable on dividends; (2) transactions that circumvent the application of the treaty rule that allows source taxation of shares of companies that derive their value primarily from immovable property; (3) situations where an entity is resident of two Contracting States, and (4) situations where the State of residence exempts the income of permanent establishments situated in third States and where shares, debt-claims, rights or property are transferred to permanent establishments set up in countries that do not tax such income or offer preferential treatment to that income.

The report recognises that the adoption of anti-abuse rules in tax treaties is not sufficient to address tax avoidance strategies that seek to circumvent provisions of domestic tax laws; these must be addressed through domestic anti-abuse rules, including through rules that will result from the work on other parts of the Action Plan. The report includes changes to the OECD Model Tax Convention aimed at ensuring that treaties do not inadvertently prevent the application of such domestic anti-abuse rules. This is done by expanding the parts of the Commentary of the OECD Model Tax Convention that already deal with this issue and by explaining that the inclusion of the PPT rule in treaties, which will incorporate the principle already included in the Commentary of the OECD Model Tax Convention, will provide a clear statement that the Contracting States intend to deny the application of the provisions of their treaties when transactions or arrangements are entered into in order to obtain the benefits of these provisions in inappropriate circumstances.

The report also addresses two specific issues related to the interaction between treaties and domestic anti-abuse rules. The first issue relates to the application of tax treaties to restrict a Contracting State's right to tax its own residents. A new rule will codify the principle that treaties do not restrict a State's right to tax its own residents (subject to certain exceptions). The second issue deals with so-called "departure" or "exit" taxes, under which liability to tax on some types of income that has accrued for the benefit of a resident (whether an individual or a legal person) is triggered in the event that the resident ceases to be a resident of that State. Changes to the Commentary of the OECD Model Tax Convention will clarify that treaties do not prevent the application of these taxes.

Section B of the report addresses the part of Action 6 that asked for clarification "that tax treaties are not intended to be used to generate double non-taxation". This clarification is provided through a reformulation of the title and preamble of the Model Tax Convention that will clearly state that the joint intention of the parties to a tax treaty is to eliminate double taxation without creating opportunities for tax evasion and avoidance, in particular through treaty shopping arrangements.

Section C of the report addresses the third part of the work mandated by Action 6, which was "to identify the tax policy considerations that, in general, countries should consider before deciding to enter into a tax treaty with another country". The policy considerations described in that section should help countries explain their decisions not to enter into tax treaties with certain low or no-tax jurisdictions; these policy considerations will also be relevant for countries that need to consider whether they should modify (or, ultimately, terminate) a treaty previously concluded in the event that a change of circumstances (such as changes to the domestic law of a treaty partner) raises BEPS concerns related to that treaty.

This final version of the report supersedes the interim version issued in September 2014. A number of changes have been made to the rules proposed in the September 2014 report. As noted at the beginning of the report, however, additional work will be required in order to fully consider proposals recently released by the United States concerning the LOB rule and other provisions included in the report. Since the United States does not anticipate finalising its new model tax treaty until the end of 2015, the relevant provisions included in this report will need to be reviewed afterwards and will therefore be finalised in the first part of 2016. An examination of the issues related to the treaty entitlement of certain types of investment funds will also continue after September 2015 with a similar deadline.

The various anti-abuse rules that are included in this report will be among the changes proposed for inclusion in the multilateral instrument that will implement the results of the work on treaty issues mandated by the OECD/G20 BEPS Project.

Introduction

1. At the request of the G20, the OECD published its *Action Plan on Base Erosion and Profit Shifting* (BEPS Action Plan, OECD, 2013) in July 2013. The BEPS Action Plan includes 15 actions to address BEPS in a comprehensive manner and sets deadlines to implement these actions.

2. The BEPS Action Plan identifies treaty abuse, and in particular treaty shopping, as one of the most important sources of BEPS concerns. Action 6 (Prevent Treaty Abuse) describes the work to be undertaken in this area. The relevant part of the Action Plan reads as follows:

> **Existing domestic and international tax rules should be modified in order to more closely align the allocation of income with the economic activity that generates that income:**
>
> ***Treaty abuse is one of the most important sources of BEPS concerns.*** The Commentary on Article 1 of the OECD Model Tax Convention already includes a number of examples of provisions that could be used to address treaty-shopping situations as well as other cases of treaty abuse, which may give rise to double non-taxation. Tight treaty anti-abuse clauses coupled with the exercise of taxing rights under domestic laws will contribute to restore source taxation in a number of cases.
>
> ***Action 6 – Prevent treaty abuse***
>
> *Develop model treaty provisions and recommendations regarding the design of domestic rules to prevent the granting of treaty benefits in inappropriate circumstances. Work will also be done to clarify that tax treaties are not intended to be used to generate double non-taxation and to identify the tax policy considerations that, in general, countries should consider before deciding to enter into a tax treaty with another country. The work will be co-ordinated with the work on hybrids.*

3. This report is the result of the work carried on in the three different areas identified by Action 6:

A. Develop model treaty provisions and recommendations regarding the design of domestic rules to prevent the granting of treaty benefits in inappropriate circumstances.

B. Clarify that tax treaties are not intended to be used to generate double non-taxation.

C. Identify the tax policy considerations that, in general, countries should consider before deciding to enter into a tax treaty with another country.

4. The conclusions of the work in these three different areas of work correspond respectively to Sections A, B and C of this report. These conclusions take the form of changes to the OECD Model Tax Convention (in this report, all changes that are proposed to the existing text of the Model Tax Convention appear in ***bold italics*** for additions and ~~strikethrough~~ for deletions).

5. These changes reflect the agreement that the OECD Model should be amended to include the minimum level of protection against treaty abuse, including treaty shopping, described in the Executive summary and paragraph 22 below, as this minimum level of protection is necessary to effectively address BEPS.

6. When examining the model treaty provisions included in this report, it is also important to note that these are model provisions that need to be adapted to the specificities of individual States and the circumstances of the negotiation of bilateral conventions. For example:

- Some countries may have constitutional restrictions or concerns based on EU law that prevent them from adopting the exact wording of the model provisions that are recommended in this report.
- Some countries may have domestic anti-abuse rules that effectively prevent some of the treaty abuses described in this report and, to the extent that these rules conform with the principles set out in this report (and, in particular, in Section A.2) and offer the minimum protection referred to in paragraph 22 below, may not need some of the rules proposed in this report.
- Similarly, the courts of some countries have developed various interpretative tools (e.g. economic substance, substance-over-form) that effectively address various forms of domestic law and treaty abuses and these countries might not require the general treaty-abuse provision included in subsection A.1(a)(ii) below or might prefer a more restricted form of that provision.
- The administrative capacity of some countries might prevent them from applying certain detailed treaty rules and might require them to opt for more general anti-abuse provisions.

For these reasons, a number of the model provisions included in this report offer alternatives and a certain degree of flexibility. There is agreement, however, that these alternatives aim to reach a common goal, i.e. to ensure that States incorporate in their treaties sufficient safeguards to prevent treaty abuse, in particular as regards treaty shopping. For that reason, the report recommends a minimum level of protection that should be implemented (see paragraph 22 below).

Further work to be done

7. Additional work needs to be done on certain issues related to the contents of this report.

8. First, at the end of May 2015, the United States released, for public comments to be sent by 15 September 2015, a new version of its limitation-on-benefits (LOB) rule and of other provisions of its model tax treaty that are similar to provisions included in this report.[1] When these new United States provisions were discussed, it was agreed that they should be further examined once finalised by the United States in the light of the comments that will be received on them. For that reason, the parts of this report that include the LOB rule, its Commentary and provisions similar to those that were released by the United States in May 2015 will need to be reviewed after the adoption of this report. The work on those provisions and the relevant part of the Commentary will be finalised in the first part of 2016, which will allow them to be considered as part of the negotiation of the multilateral instrument that will implement the results of the work on treaty issues mandated by the BEPS Action Plan.

9. Second, paragraph 5 of the previous version of this report indicated that further work was needed with respect to the policy considerations relevant to the treaty entitlement of collective investment vehicles (CIVs) and non-CIV funds. As a result of the follow-up work on these issues and of the comments received from stakeholders, it was concluded that there was general support for the conclusions included in the 2010 OECD Report "*The Granting of Treaty Benefits with Respect to the Income of Collective Investment Vehicles*" and that since subparagraph 2 *f)* of the LOB rule included in this report dealt with the application of the LOB to CIVs in a way that reflected the conclusions of the 2010 CIV Report, there was no need for additional changes to the report on Action 6 in order to address issues related to collective investment vehicles, even though it was also agreed that the implementation of the recommendations of the TRACE project were important for the practical application of these conclusions.

10. The same conclusion could not be reached, however, as regards the policy considerations relevant to the treaty entitlement of non-CIV funds and further work is needed in that area.

11. That work will first confirm the conclusions of the 2008 OECD report "*Tax Treaty Issues Related to REITs*", which deals with the treaty entitlement of Real Estate Investment Trusts (REITs). Whilst the conclusions of the 2010 CIV Report have been confirmed as part of the work on Action 6, this has not been done with respect to the 2008 REIT Report. It is therefore agreed to make the following change in the final version of the Commentary of the LOB rule to be produced in 2016:

*Add the following footnote to the first part of paragraph 31 of the Commentary on subparagraph 2 f) of the LOB rule included in paragraph 16 of the Report on Action 6 (the additional footnote appears in **bold italics**):*

> 31. As indicated in the footnote to subparagraph *f)*, whether a specific rule concerning collective investment vehicles (CIVs) should be included in paragraph 2, and, if so, how that rule should be drafted, will depend on how the Convention applies to CIVs and on the treatment and use of CIVs in each Contracting State.[1] ***Whilst no such rule will be needed with respect to an entity that would otherwise constitute a "qualified person" under other parts of paragraph 2***, ~~Such~~ a specific rule will frequently be needed since a CIV may not be ~~a qualified person~~ ***entitled to treaty benefits*** under either the other provisions of paragraph 2 or ***under paragraph*** 3, because, in many cases…
>
> [*Footnote 1*] ***See also paragraphs 67.1 to 67.7 of the Commentary on Article 10 and the report "Tax Treaty Issues Related to REITs" which deal with the treaty entitlement of Real Estate Investment Trusts (REITs). With respect to the application of the definition of "resident of a Contracting State" to REITs, see paragraphs 8-9 of the report "Tax Treaty Issues Related to REITs".***

12. Additional work will also ensure that a pension fund should be considered to be a resident of the State in which it is constituted regardless of whether that pension fund benefits from a limited or complete exemption from taxation in that State. This will be done through changes to the OECD Model Tax Convention, to be also finalised in the first part of 2016, that will ensure that outcome for funds that will meet a definition of "recognised pension fund" which will likely include the following elements:

- the definition will refer to entities or arrangement established in a State and constituted and operated exclusively or almost exclusively to administer or provide retirement or similar benefits to individuals;

- the entities or arrangements to which the definition will apply will need to be treated as separate persons under the taxation laws of that State;
- in order to cover only funds that the tax law recognises as pension funds, these entities will need to be regulated as pensions funds by the State in which they are established;
- the definition will also need to cover entities and arrangements that are constituted and operated exclusively or almost exclusively to invest funds for the benefit of entities or arrangements that will themselves qualify as "recognised pension funds".

13. That definition will need to be accompanied by detailed Commentary that will explain some of these requirements, in particular the requirement that a pension fund "be regulated as such". Consultation with stakeholders will be necessary to ensure that the definition and its Commentary cover the main forms of pension funds that currently exist.

14. As regards the broader question of the treaty entitlement of non-CIV funds, the OECD recognises the economic importance of these funds and the need to ensure that treaty benefits be granted where appropriate. The new treaty provision on transparent entities that is included in Part 2 of the Report on Action 2 (*Neutralising the Effects of Hybrid Mismatch Arrangements*, OECD, 2015a) will be beneficial for non-CIV funds that use entities that one or the two Contracting States treat as fiscally transparent since income derived through such entities that will be taxed in the hands of the investors in these entities will generally receive treaty entitlement at the level of these investors even if these investors are residents of third States. Also, the possible inclusion of a derivative benefits provision in the LOB rule to be finalised in the first part of 2016 will likely also address some of the concerns regarding the treaty entitlement of non-CIV funds in which there are non-resident investors. Notwithstanding this, however, there is a need to continue to examine issues related to the treaty entitlement of non-CIV funds to ensure that the new treaty provisions that are being considered adequately address the treaty entitlement of non-CIVs. The continued examination of these issues would also address two general concerns that governments have about granting treaty benefits with respect to non-CIVs: that non-CIVs may be used to provide treaty benefits to investors that are not themselves entitled to treaty benefits and that investors may defer recognition of income on which treaty benefits have been granted. This work, which will also benefit from consultation with stakeholders, will need to be completed in the first part of 2016 in order to be relevant for the negotiation of the multilateral instrument.

A. Treaty provisions and/or domestic rules to prevent the granting of treaty benefits in inappropriate circumstances

15. In order to determine the best way to prevent the granting of treaty benefits in inappropriate circumstances, it was found useful to distinguish two types of cases:

1. Cases where a person tries to circumvent limitations provided by the treaty itself.
2. Cases where a person tries to circumvent the provisions of domestic tax law using treaty benefits.

16. Since the first category of cases involve situations where a person seeks to circumvent rules that are specific to tax treaties, it is unlikely that these cases will be addressed by specific anti-abuse rules found in domestic law. Although a domestic general anti-abuse rule could prevent the granting of treaty benefits in these cases, a more direct approach involves the drafting of anti-abuse rules to be included in treaties. The situation is different in the second category of cases: since these cases involve the avoidance of domestic law, they cannot be addressed exclusively through treaty provisions and require domestic anti-abuse rules, which raises the issue of the interaction between tax treaties and these domestic rules.

1. Cases where a person tries to circumvent limitations provided by the treaty itself

a) Treaty shopping

17. The first requirement that must be met by a person who seeks to obtain benefits under a tax treaty is that the person must be "a resident of a Contracting State", as defined in Article 4 of the OECD Model Tax Convention. There are a number of arrangements through which a person who is not a resident of a Contracting State may attempt to obtain benefits that a tax treaty grants to a resident of that State. These arrangements are generally referred to as "treaty shopping". Treaty shopping cases typically involve persons who are residents of third States attempting to access indirectly the benefits of a treaty between two Contracting States.[2]

18. The OECD has previously examined the issue of treaty shopping in different contexts:

- The concept of "beneficial owner" was introduced in the Model Tax Convention in 1977 in order to deal with simple treaty shopping situations where income is paid to an intermediary resident of a treaty country who is not treated as the owner of that income for tax purposes (such as an agent or nominee). At the same time, a short new section on "Improper Use of the Convention" (which included two examples of treaty shopping) was added to the Commentary on Article 1 and the Committee indicated that it intended "to make an in-depth study of such problems and of other ways of dealing with them".

- That in-depth study resulted in the 1986 reports on Double Taxation and the Use of Base companies and Double Taxation and the Use of Conduit Companies,[3] the issue of treaty shopping being primarily dealt with in the latter report.
- In 1992, as a result of the report on Double Taxation and the Use of Conduit Companies, various examples of provisions dealing with different aspects of treaty shopping were added to the section on "Improper Use of the Convention" in the Commentary on Article 1. These included the alternative provisions currently found in paragraphs 13 to 19 of the Commentary on Article 1 under the heading "Conduit company cases".
- In 2003, as a result of the report Restricting the Entitlement to Treaty Benefits[4] (which was prepared as a follow-up to the 1998 Report Harmful Tax Competition: an Emerging Global Issue),[5] new paragraphs intended to clarify the meaning of "beneficial owner" in some conduit situations were added to the Commentary on Articles 10, 11 and 12 and the section on "Improper Use of the Convention" was substantially extended to include additional examples of anti-abuse rules, including a comprehensive limitation-on-benefits provision based on the provision found in the 1996 US Model[6] as well as a purpose-based anti-abuse provision based on UK practice and applicable to Articles 10, 11, 12 and 21.[7]
- Finally, additional work on the clarification of the "beneficial owner" concept, which resulted in changes to the Commentary on Articles 10, 11 and 12 that were included in the Model Tax Convention through the 2014 Update, has allowed the OECD to examine the limits of using that concept as a tool to address various treaty-shopping situations. As indicated in paragraph 12.5 of the Commentary on Article 10, "[w]hilst the concept of 'beneficial owner' deals with some forms of tax avoidance (i.e. those involving the interposition of a recipient who is obliged to pass on the dividend to someone else), it does not deal with other cases of treaty shopping and must not, therefore, be considered as restricting in any way the application of other approaches to addressing such cases."

19. A review of the treaty practices of OECD and non-OECD countries shows that countries use different approaches to try to address treaty shopping cases not already dealt with by the provisions of the Model Tax Convention. Based on the advantages and limitations of these approaches, it is recommended that the following three-pronged approach be used to address treaty shopping situations:

- First, a clear statement that the Contracting States, when entering into a treaty, wish to prevent tax avoidance and, in particular, intend to avoid creating opportunities for treaty shopping will be included in tax treaties (see Section B of this report).
- Second, a specific anti-abuse rule based on the limitation-on-benefits provisions included in treaties concluded by the United States and a few other countries (the "LOB rule") will be included in the OECD Model. Such a specific rule will address a large number of treaty shopping situations based on the legal nature, ownership in, and general activities of, residents of a Contracting State (see subsection A.1(a)(i) below).
- Third, in order to address other forms of treaty abuse, including treaty shopping situations that would not be covered by the LOB rule described in the preceding bullet point (such as certain conduit financing arrangements), a more general anti-abuse rule based on the principal purposes of transactions or arrangements (the principal purposes test or "PPT" rule) will be included in the OECD Model. That

rule will incorporate the principles already reflected in paragraphs 9.5, 22, 22.1 and 22.2 of the Commentary on Article 1, according to which the benefits of a tax treaty should not be available where one of the principal purposes of arrangements or transactions is to secure a benefit under a tax treaty and obtaining that benefit in these circumstances would be contrary to the object and purpose of the relevant provisions of the tax treaty (see subsection A.1(a)(ii) below).

20. The combination of the LOB and the PPT rules described above recognises that each rule has strengths and weaknesses. For instance, the various provisions of the LOB rule are based on objective criteria that provide more certainty than the PPT rule, which requires a case-by-case analysis based on what can reasonably be considered to be one of the principal purposes of transactions or arrangements. For that reason, the LOB rule is useful as a specific anti-abuse rule aimed at treaty shopping situations that can be identified on the basis of criteria based on the legal nature, ownership in, and general activities of, certain entities. The LOB rule, however, only focusses on treaty shopping and does not address other forms of treaty abuses; it also does not address certain forms of treaty shopping, such as conduit financing arrangements, through which a resident of Contracting State that would otherwise qualify for treaty benefits is used as an intermediary by persons who are not entitled to these benefits.

21. The combination of an LOB rule and a PPT rule may not be appropriate or necessary for all countries. For instance, as mentioned in paragraph 6 above, some countries may have domestic anti-abuse rules, or the courts of some countries may have developed various interpretative tools (e.g. economic substance or substance-over-form), that effectively address various forms of domestic law and treaty abuses and these countries might not require the general treaty anti-abuse provision included in subsection A.1(a)(ii) below or might prefer a more restricted form of that provision. It is also recognised that the LOB rule will need to be adapted to reflect certain constraints or policy choices concerning other aspects of a bilateral tax treaty between two Contracting States (e.g. constitutional restrictions or concerns based on EU law or policy choices concerning the treatment of collective investment vehicles).

22. As long as the approach that countries adopt effectively addresses treaty abuses along the lines of this report, some flexibility is therefore possible. At a minimum, however, countries should agree to include in their tax treaties an express statement that their common intention is to eliminate double taxation without creating opportunities for non-taxation or reduced taxation through tax evasion or avoidance, including through treaty shopping arrangements (see Section B); they should also implement that common intention through either the combined approach described in paragraph 19 (subject to the necessary adaptations referred to in paragraph 6 above), the inclusion of the PPT rule or the inclusion of the LOB rule supplemented by a mechanism (such as a treaty rule that might take the form of a PPT rule restricted to conduit arrangements or domestic anti-abuse rules or judicial doctrines that would achieve a similar result) that would deal with conduit arrangements not already dealt with in tax treaties.

23. Countries commit to adopt in their bilateral treaties measures that implement the minimum standard described in the preceding paragraph if requested to do so by other countries that have made the same commitment and that will request the inclusion of these measures. Whilst the way in which this minimum standard will be implemented in each bilateral treaty will need to be agreed to between the Contracting States, this commitment applies to existing and future treaties. Since the conclusion of a new treaty and the modification of an existing treaty depend on the overall balance of the provisions

of a treaty, however, this commitment should not be interpreted as a commitment to conclude new treaties or amend existing treaties within a specified period of time. Also, if a country is not itself concerned by the effect of treaty-shopping on its own taxation rights as a State of source, it will not be obliged to apply provisions such as the LOB or the PPT as long as it agrees to include in a treaty provisions that its treaty partner will be able to use for that purpose. Whilst the minimum standard will be included in the multilateral instrument that will be negotiated pursuant to Action 15 of the BEPS Action Plan, which will provide an effective way to implement it swiftly, this may not be sufficient to ensure its implementation since participation in the multilateral instrument is not mandatory and two countries that are parties to an existing treaty may have different preferences as to how the minimum standard should be met; monitoring of the implementation of the minimum standard will therefore be necessary.

24. Other changes included in this report will also assist in preventing treaty shopping. For instance, the new specific treaty anti-abuse rules included in subsection A.1(b) will deal with some specific forms of treaty shopping, such as strategies aimed at using a permanent establishment located in a low-tax jurisdiction in order to take advantage of the exemption method applicable by a Contracting State. Section C, which includes tax policy considerations that, in general, States should consider before deciding to enter into a tax treaty with another country, may also contribute to the reduction of treaty shopping opportunities. Conversely, the approach described in paragraph 19 above is not restricted to treaty shopping cases and will also contribute to preventing the granting of treaty benefits in other inappropriate circumstances, this being particularly the case of the general treaty anti-abuse provision referred to at the end of that paragraph.

i) Limitation-on-benefits rule

25. As indicated in paragraph 19, a specific anti-abuse rule aimed at treaty shopping, the LOB rule, will be included in the OECD Model. That rule will be based on provisions already found in a number of tax treaties, including primarily treaties concluded by the United States but also some treaties concluded by Japan and India. The detailed LOB provisions and related Commentary included below reflect the detailed provision that was included in the first version of this report released in September 2014 as modified as a result of subsequent work on various aspects of that provision, including the addition of a simplified version of the rule released in May 2015. At the end of May 2015, however, the United States released a new version of the LOB rule included in its model treaty[8] for public comments to be sent by 15 September 2015. When that new version was discussed, it was agreed that it should be further examined once finalised by the United States in the light of the comments that will be received on it. For that reason, the detailed LOB provisions below and the Commentary on these provisions will need to be reviewed. The simplified LOB provisions will also require further work and Commentary on those provisions will be drafted. The final version of the provisions and the Commentary will be produced in the first part of 2016, which will allow the new provisions to be considered as part of the negotiation of the multilateral instrument that will implement the results of the work on treaty issues mandated by the BEPS Action Plan. The following should therefore be considered as a draft subject to changes:

ARTICLE X

ENTITLEMENT TO BENEFITS[9]

[1.[10] [Provision that would deny treaty benefits to a resident of a Contracting State who is not a "qualified person" as defined in paragraph 2]

2. [Definition of situations where a resident would be a qualified person, which would cover

a) an individual;

b) a Contracting State, its political subdivisions and entities that it wholly owns;

c) certain publicly-listed entities and their affiliates

d) certain charities and pension funds

e) other entities that meet certain ownership requirements

f) certain collective investment vehicles]

3. [Provision that would provide treaty benefits to certain income derived by a person that is not a qualified person if the person is engaged in the active conduct of a business in its State of residence and the income is derived in connection with, or is incidental to, that business]

4. [Provision that would provide treaty benefits to a person that is not a qualified person if at least more than an agreed proportion of that entity is owned by certain persons entitled to equivalent benefits]

5. [Provision that would allow the competent authority of a Contracting State to grant certain treaty benefits to a person where benefits would otherwise be denied under paragraphs 1 to 4]

6. [Definitions applicable for the purposes of paragraphs 1 to 5]

Add the following new Commentary on Article [X] to the Commentary of the OECD Model Tax Convention:

[COMMENTARY ON ARTICLE [X] CONCERNING THE ENTITLEMENT TO TREATY BENEFITS

Preliminary remarks

1. As explained in the footnote to the Article, Article [X] reflects the intention of the Contracting States to eliminate double taxation without creating opportunities for non-taxation or reduced taxation through tax evasion or avoidance, including through treaty shopping arrangements. The drafting of this Article will depend on how the Contracting States decide to do so. Depending on their own circumstances, States may wish to adopt only the general anti-abuse rule of paragraph 7 of the Article, may prefer instead to adopt the detailed version of paragraphs 1 to 6 that is described below, which they would supplement by a mechanism that would address specific conduit arrangements, or may prefer to

include in their treaty the general anti-abuse rule of paragraph 7 together with any variation of paragraphs 1 to 6 described below.

2. A State may prefer the last approach described above because it combines the flexibility of a general rule that can prevent a large number of abusive transactions with the certainty of a more "automatic" rule that prevent transactions that are known to cause treaty shopping concerns and that can be easily described by reference to certain features (such as the foreign ownership of an entity). That last approach is reflected in the "simplified version" of paragraphs 1 to 6 reproduced below, which should only be used in combination with the general rule of paragraph 7. Such a combination should not be construed in any way as restricting the scope of the general anti-abuse rule of paragraph 7: a transaction or arrangement should not be considered to be outside the scope of paragraph 7 simply because the specific anti-abuse rules of paragraphs 1 to 6, which only deal with certain cases of treaty shopping that can be easily identified by certain of their features, are not applicable.

3. A State may, however, prefer to deal with treaty-shopping without the general anti-abuse rule of paragraph 7, relying instead on the specific anti-abuse rules of paragraphs 1 to 6, together with a mechanism that will address conduit arrangements that would escape the application of these paragraphs. This may be the case of a State whose domestic law includes strong anti-abuse rules that are sufficient to deal with other forms of treaty abuses. States that adopt that approach will need to ensure that the version of paragraph 1 to 6 that they include in their bilateral conventions is sufficiently robust to prevent most forms of treaty shopping. For this reason, the paragraphs below provide different versions of the provisions of paragraphs 1 to 6, the more robust version of these paragraphs mentioned above being referred to as the "detailed version". States that do not wish to include paragraph 7 for the reasons explained in this paragraph should adopt the detailed version, as opposed to the "simplified" version, subject to any adaptations referred to in the Commentary below.

3.1 This Article contains provisions that are intended to prevent various forms of treaty shopping through which persons who are not residents of a Contracting State might establish an entity that would be a resident of that State in order to reduce or eliminate taxation in the other Contracting State through the benefits of the tax treaty concluded between these two States. Allowing persons who are not directly entitled to treaty benefits (such as the reduction or elimination of withholding taxes on dividends, interest or royalties) to obtain these benefits indirectly through treaty shopping would frustrate the bilateral and reciprocal nature of tax treaties. If, for instance, a State knows that its residents can indirectly access the benefits of treaties concluded by another State, it may have little interest in granting reciprocal benefits to residents of that other State through the conclusion of a tax treaty. Also, in such a case, the benefits that would be indirectly obtained may not be appropriate given the nature of the tax system of the former State; if, for instance, that State does not levy an income tax on a certain type of income, it would be inappropriate for its residents to benefit from the provisions of a tax treaty concluded between two other States that grant a reduction or elimination of source taxation for that type of income and that were designed on the assumption that the two Contracting States would tax such income.

3.2 The provisions of the Article seek to deny treaty benefits in the case of structures that typically result in the indirect granting of treaty benefits to persons that are not directly entitled to these benefits whilst recognising that in some cases, persons who are not residents of a Contracting State may establish an entity in that State for legitimate business reasons. Although these provisions apply regardless of whether or not a particular structure was adopted for treaty-shopping purposes, the Article allows the competent authority of a Contracting State to grant treaty benefits where the other provisions of the Article would otherwise deny these benefits but the competent authority determines that the structure did not have as one of its principal purposes the obtaining of benefits under the Convention.

3.3 The Article restricts the general scope of Article 1, according to which the Convention applies to persons who are residents of a Contracting State. Paragraph 1 of the Article provides that a resident of a Contracting State shall not be entitled to the benefits of the Convention unless it constitutes a "qualified person" under paragraph 2 or unless benefits are granted under the provisions of paragraphs 3, 4 or 5. Paragraph 2 determines who constitutes a "qualified person" by reference to the nature or attributes of various categories of persons; any person to which that paragraph applies is entitled to all the benefits of the Convention. Under paragraph 3, a person is entitled to the benefits of the Convention with respect to an item of income even if it does not constitute a "qualified person" under paragraph 2 as long as that item of income is derived in connection with the active conduct of a trade or business in that person's State of residence (subject to certain exceptions). Paragraph 4 is a "derivative benefits" rule that allows certain entities owned by residents of third States to obtain treaty benefits provided that these residents would have been entitled to equivalent benefits if they had invested directly. Paragraph 5 includes the provisions that allow the competent authority of a Contracting State to grant treaty benefits where the other provisions of the Article would otherwise deny these benefits. Paragraph 6 includes a number of definitions that apply for the purposes of the Article.

Provision denying treaty benefits to a resident of a Contracting State who is not a "qualified person"

Simplified version

1. Except as otherwise provided in this Article, a resident of a Contracting State shall be entitled to the benefits that would otherwise be accorded by this Convention only if such resident is a qualified person.

Detailed version

1. Except as otherwise provided in this Article, a resident of a Contracting State shall not be entitled to a benefit that would otherwise be accorded by this Convention (other than a benefit under paragraph 3 of Article 4, paragraph 2 of Article 9 or Article 25), unless such resident is a "qualified person", as defined in paragraph 2, at the time that the benefit would be accorded.

Commentary on the detailed version

4. Paragraph 1 provides that a resident of a Contracting State, as defined under Article 4, will be entitled to the benefits otherwise accorded to residents of a Contracting State under the Convention only if it constitutes a "qualified person" under paragraph 2 or unless benefits are otherwise granted under paragraphs 3, 4 or 5. The benefits otherwise accorded to a resident of a Contracting State under the Convention include all limitations to the Contracting States' taxing rights under Articles 6 through 21, the elimination of double taxation provided by Article 23 and the protection afforded to residents of a Contracting State under Article 24. The Article does not, however, restrict the availability of treaty benefits under paragraph 3 of Article 4, paragraph 2 of Article 9 or Article 25 or under the few provisions of the Convention that do not require that a person be a resident of Contracting State in order to enjoy the benefits of those provisions (e.g. the provisions of paragraph 1 of Article 24, to the extent that they apply to nationals who are not residents of either Contracting State).

5. Paragraph 1 does not extend in any way the scope of the benefits granted by the Convention. Thus, a resident of a Contracting State who constitutes a "qualified person" under paragraph 2 must still meet the conditions of the other provisions of the Convention in order to obtain these benefits (e.g. that resident must be the beneficial owner of dividends in order to benefit from the provisions of paragraph 2 of Article 10) and these benefits may be denied or restricted under applicable anti-abuse rules.

6. Paragraph 1 applies at any time when the Convention would otherwise provide a benefit to a resident of a Contracting State. Thus, for example, it applies at the time when income to which Article 6 applies is derived by a resident of a Contracting State, at the time that dividends to which Article 10 applies are paid to a resident of a Contracting State or at any time when profits to which Article 7 applies are made. The paragraph requires that, in order to be entitled to the benefit provided by the relevant provision of the Convention, the resident of the Contracting State must be a "qualified person", within the meaning of paragraph 2, at the relevant time. In some cases, however, the definition of "qualified person" requires that a resident of a Contracting State must satisfy certain conditions over a period of time in order to constitute a "qualified person" at a given time.

Situations where a resident is a qualified person

Simplified version

2. For the purposes of this Article, a resident of a Contracting State shall be a qualified person if the resident is either:

Detailed version

2. A resident of a Contracting State shall be a qualified person at a time when a benefit would otherwise be accorded by the Convention if, at that time, the resident is:

Commentary on the detailed version

7. Paragraph 2 has six subparagraphs, each of which describes a category of residents that are qualified persons.

8. It is intended that the provisions of paragraph 2 will be self-executing. Unlike the provisions of paragraph 5, discussed below, claiming benefits under paragraph 2 does not require advance competent authority ruling or approval. The tax authorities may, of course, on review, determine that the taxpayer has improperly interpreted the paragraph and is not entitled to the benefits claimed.

Individuals

a) an individual;

9. Subparagraph 2 a) provides that any individual who is a resident of a Contracting State will be a qualified person. As explained in paragraph 35 below, under some treaty provisions, a collective investment vehicle must be treated as an individual for the purposes of applying the relevant treaty; where that is the case, such a collective investment vehicle will therefore constitute a qualified person by virtue of subparagraph a).

Governments

Simplified version

b) that Contracting State, any political subdivision or local authority thereof, the central bank thereof or a person that is wholly owned, directly or indirectly, by that State or any political subdivision or local authority thereof;

Detailed version

b) a Contracting State, or a political subdivision or local authority thereof, or a person that is wholly-owned by such State, political subdivision or local authority;

Commentary on the detailed version

10. Subparagraph 2 b) provides that the Contracting States and any political subdivision or local authority thereof constitute qualified persons. The subparagraph applies to any part of a State, such as an agency or instrumentality that does not constitute a separate person. The last part of the subparagraph provides that a separate legal person which constitutes a resident of a Contracting State and is wholly-owned by a Contracting State, or a political subdivision or local authority thereof, will also be a qualified person and, therefore, will be entitled to all the benefits of the Convention whilst it qualifies as such. The wording of the subparagraph may need to be adapted to reflect the different legal nature that State-owned entities, such as sovereign wealth funds, may have in the Contracting States as well as the different views that these States may have concerning the application of Article 4 to these entities (see paragraphs 6.35 to 6.39 of the Commentary on Article 1 and paragraphs 8.5 to 8.7 of the Commentary on Article 4).

Publicly-traded companies and entities

__Simplified version__

__c) a company, if the principal class of its shares is regularly traded on one or more recognised stock exchanges;__

__d) a person other than a company, if its beneficial interests are regularly traded on one or more recognised stock exchanges;__

__Detailed version__

__c) a company or other entity, if, throughout the taxable period that includes that time__

__i) the principal class of its shares (and any disproportionate class of shares) is regularly traded on one or more recognised stock exchanges, and either:__

__A) its principal class of shares is primarily traded on one or more recognised stock exchanges located in the Contracting State of which the company or entity is a resident; or__

__B) the company's or entity's primary place of management and control is in the Contracting State of which it is a resident; or__

__ii) at least 50 per cent of the aggregate voting power and value of the shares (and at least 50 per cent of any disproportionate class of shares) in the company or entity is owned directly or indirectly by five or fewer companies or entities entitled to benefits under subdivision i) of this subparagraph, [provided that, in the case of indirect ownership, each intermediate owner is a resident of either Contracting State];__

Commentary on the detailed version

11. Subparagraph c) recognises that, as a general rule, because the shares of publicly-traded companies and of some entities are generally widely-held, these companies and entities are unlikely to be established for treaty shopping. The provisions of subdivision i) apply to publicly-traded companies and entities and the provisions of subdivision ii) apply to subsidiaries of publicly-traded companies and entities. As indicated in subparagraph h) of paragraph 6, for the purposes of subparagraph c), the term "shares" covers comparable interests in entities, other than companies, to which the subparagraph applies; this includes, for example, publicly-traded units of a trust.

12. Subdivision i) provides that a company or entity resident in a Contracting State constitutes a qualified person at a time when a benefit is provided by the Convention if, throughout the taxable period that includes that time, the principal class of its shares, and any disproportionate class of shares, is regularly traded on one or more recognised stock exchanges, provided that the company or entity also satisfies at least one of the following additional requirements: first, the company's or entity's principal class of shares is primarily traded on one or more recognised stock exchanges located in the Contracting State of which the company or entity is a resident or, second, the company's or entity's primary place of management and control is in its State of residence. These additional

requirements take account of the fact that whilst a publicly-traded company or entity may be technically resident in a given State, it may not have a sufficient relationship with that State to justify allowing such a company or entity to obtain the benefits of treaties concluded by that State. Such a sufficient relationship may be established by the fact that the shares of the publicly-traded company or entity are primarily traded in recognised stock exchanges situated in the State of residence of the company or entity; given the fact that the globalisation of financial markets means that shares of publicly-listed companies that are residents of some States are often traded on foreign stock exchanges, the alternative test provides that this sufficient relationship may also be established by the fact that the company or entity is primarily managed and controlled in its State of residence.

13. A company or entity whose principal class of shares is regularly traded on a recognised stock exchange will nevertheless not qualify for benefits under subparagraph c) of paragraph 2 if it has a disproportionate class of shares that is not regularly traded on a recognised stock exchange.

14. The terms "recognised stock exchange", "principal class of shares" and "disproportionate class of shares" are defined in paragraph 6 (see below). As indicated in these definitions, the principal class of shares of a company must be determined after excluding special voting shares which are issued as a means of establishing a "dual listed company arrangement", which is also defined in paragraph 6.

15. The regular trading requirement can be met by trading of issued shares on any recognised exchange or exchanges located in either State. Trading on one or more recognised stock exchanges may be aggregated for purposes of this requirement; a company or entity could therefore satisfy this requirement if its shares are regularly traded, in whole or in part, on a recognised stock exchange located in the other Contracting State.

16. Subdivision (i)A) includes the additional requirement that the shares of the company or entity be primarily traded in one or more recognised stock exchanges located in the State of residence of the company or entity. In general, the principal class of shares of a company or entity are "primarily traded" on one or more recognised stock exchanges located in the State of residence of that company or entity if, during the relevant taxation year, the number of shares in the company's or entity's principal class of shares that are traded on these stock exchanges exceeds the number of shares in the company's or entity's principal class of shares that are traded on established securities markets in any other State. Some States, however, consider that the fact that shares of a company or entity resident in a Contracting State are primarily traded on recognised stock exchanges situated in other States (e.g. in a State that is part of the European Economic Area within which rules relating to stock exchanges and securities create a single market for securities trading) constitutes a sufficient safeguard against the use of that company or entity for treaty-shopping purposes; States that share that view may modify subdivision (i)A) accordingly.

17. Subdivision (i)B) provides the alternative requirement applicable to a company or entity whose principal class of shares is regularly traded on recognised stock exchanges but not primarily traded on recognised stock exchanges situated in the State of residence of the company or entity. Such a company or entity may claim treaty benefits if its "primary place of management and control" (as defined in subparagraph d) of paragraph 6) is in its State of residence.

18. The conditions of subparagraph c) must be satisfied throughout the taxable period of the company or entity. This does not require that the shares of the company or entity be traded on the relevant stock exchanges each day of the relevant period. For shares to be considered as regularly traded on one or more stock exchanges throughout the taxable period, it is necessary that more than a very small percentage of the shares be actively traded during a sufficiently large number of days included in that period. The test would be met, for example, if 10 per cent of the average number of outstanding shares of a given class of shares of a company were traded during 60 days of trading taking place in the taxable period of the company. The phrase "taxable period" in subparagraphs c) and e) refers to the period for which an annual tax return must be filed in the State of residence of the company or entity. If the Contracting States have a concept corresponding to "taxable period" in their domestic law, such as "taxable year", they are free to replace the reference to taxable period by that other concept.

19. A company resident in a Contracting State is entitled to all the benefits of the Convention under subdivision ii) of subparagraph c) of paragraph 2 if five or fewer publicly-traded companies described in subdivision i) are the direct or indirect owners of at least 50 per cent of the aggregate vote and value of the company's shares (and at least 50 per cent of any disproportionate class of shares). If the publicly-traded companies are indirect owners, however, each of the intermediate companies must be a resident of one of the Contracting States. Some States, however, consider that this last requirement is unduly restrictive and prefer to omit it.

20. Thus, for example, a company that is a resident of a Contracting State, all the shares of which are owned by another company that is a resident of the same State, would qualify for benefits under the Convention if the principal class of shares (and any disproportionate classes of shares) of the parent company are regularly and primarily traded on a recognised stock exchange in that Contracting State. Such a subsidiary would not qualify for benefits under subdivision ii), however, if the publicly-traded parent company were a resident of a third State, for example, and not a resident of one of the Contracting States. Furthermore, if a parent company in one of the Contracting States indirectly owned the bottom-tier company through a chain of subsidiaries, each such subsidiary in the chain, as an intermediate owner, must be a resident of either Contracting State in order for the subsidiary to meet the test in subdivision ii). As explained in the previous paragraph, however, some States consider that, in the case of publicly-listed companies, the condition that each subsidiary in the chain must be a resident of either Contracting State is not necessary in order to prevent treaty shopping; these States therefore prefer to omit that additional condition.

Charitable organisations and pension funds

Detailed version

d) a person, other than an individual, that

i) is a [list of the relevant non-profit organisations found in each Contracting State],

ii) is a recognised pension fund, provided that more than 50 per cent of the beneficial interests in that person are owned by individuals resident of either Contracting State, or more than [__ per cent] of the beneficial interests in that person are owned by individuals resident of either Contracting State or of any other State with respect to which the following conditions are met

A) individuals who are residents of that other State are entitled to the benefits of a comprehensive convention for the avoidance of double taxation between that other State and the State from which the benefits of this Convention are claimed, and

B) with respect to income referred to in Articles 10 and 11 of this Convention, if the person were a resident of that other State entitled to all the benefits of that other convention, the person would be entitled, under such convention, to a rate of tax with respect to the particular class of income for which benefits are being claimed under this Convention that is at least as low as the rate applicable under this Convention; or

iii) was constituted and is operated to invest funds for the benefit of persons referred to in subdivision ii), provided that substantially all the income of that person is derived from investments made for the benefit of these persons;

Commentary on the detailed version

21. Subparagraph 2 d) provides rules under which certain non-profit organisations and pension funds that qualify as resident of a Contracting State (see paragraphs 8.6 and 8.7 of the Commentary on Article 4) will be entitled to all the benefits of the Convention.

22. Entities listed in subdivision i) automatically qualify for treaty benefits without regard to the residence of their beneficiaries or members. These entities would generally correspond to those that are exempt from tax in their State of residence and that are constituted and operated exclusively to fulfil certain social functions (e.g. charitable, scientific, artistic, cultural, or educational).

23. Under subdivision ii), a resident pension fund will qualify for treaty benefits if more than 50 per cent of the beneficial interests in that person are owned by individuals resident of either Contracting State or if more than a certain percentage of these beneficial interests, to be determined during bilateral negotiations, are owned by such residents or by individuals who are residents of third States provided that, in the latter case, two additional conditions are met: first, these individuals are entitled to the benefits of a comprehensive tax convention concluded between that third State and the State of source and, second, that convention provides for a similar or greater reduction of source taxes on interest and dividends derived by pension funds of that third State. For purposes of this provision, the term "beneficial interests in that person" should be understood to refer to the interests held by persons entitled to receive pension benefits from the fund. Some States, however, consider that the risk of treaty shopping by recognised pension funds does not warrant the costs of compliance inherent in requiring funds to identify the treaty residence and entitlement of the

individuals entitled to receive pension benefits. States that share that view may modify subdivision (ii) accordingly.

24. Subdivision iii) constitutes an extension of the rule of subdivision ii) applicable to pension funds. It applies to so-called "funds of funds", which are funds which do not directly provide pension benefits to residents of either Contracting State but are constituted and operated to invest funds of pension funds that are themselves pension funds qualifying for benefits under subdivision ii). Subdivision iii) only applies, however, if substantially all the income of such a "fund of funds" is derived from investments made for the benefit of pension funds qualifying for benefits under subdivision ii).

Ownership / Base Erosion

<u>Simplified version</u>

<u>e) a person other than an individual, provided that persons who are residents of that Contracting State and are qualified persons by reason of subparagraphs a) to d) own, directly or indirectly, more than 50 per cent of the beneficial interests of the person</u>

<u>Detailed version</u>

<u>e) a person other than an individual, if</u>

<u>i) on at least half the days of the taxable period, persons who are residents of that Contracting State and that are entitled to the benefits of this Convention under subparagraph a), b) or d), or subdivision i) of subparagraph c), of this paragraph own, directly or indirectly, shares representing at least 50 per cent of the aggregate voting power and value (and at least 50 per cent of any disproportionate class of shares) of the person, [provided that, in the case of indirect ownership, each intermediate owner is a resident of that Contracting State], and</u>

<u>ii) less than 50 per cent of the person's gross income for the taxable period, as determined in the person's Contracting State of residence, is paid or accrued, directly or indirectly, to persons who are not residents of either Contracting State entitled to the benefits of this Convention under subparagraph a), b) or d), or subdivision i) of subparagraph c), of this paragraph in the form of payments that are deductible for purposes of the taxes covered by this Convention in the person's Contracting State of residence (but not including arm's length payments in the ordinary course of business for services or tangible property);</u>

Commentary on the detailed version

25. Subparagraph 2 e) provides an additional method to qualify for treaty benefits that applies to any form of legal entity that is a resident of a Contracting State. The test provided in subparagraph e), the so-called ownership and base erosion test, is a two-part test; both parts must be satisfied for the resident to be entitled to treaty benefits under subparagraph 2 e).

26. Under subdivision i), which is the ownership part of the test, 50 per cent or more of each class of shares in the person must be owned, directly or indirectly, on at least half the days of the person's taxable period, by persons who are residents of the Contracting State of which that person is a resident and that are themselves entitled to treaty benefits under subparagraphs a), b) or d), or subdivision i) of subparagraph c). In the case of indirect owners, however, each of the intermediate owners must be a resident of that Contracting State. Some States, however, consider that this last requirement is unduly restrictive and prefer to omit it.

27. Whilst subdivision i) will typically be relevant in the case of private companies, it may also apply to an entity such as a trust that is a resident of a Contracting State and that otherwise satisfies the requirements of this subdivision. According to subparagraph h) of paragraph 6, the reference to "shares", in the case of entities that are not companies, means interests that are comparable to shares; this would generally be the case of the beneficial interests in a trust. For the purposes of subdivision i), the beneficial interests in a trust will be considered to be owned by its beneficiaries in proportion to each beneficiary's actuarial interest in the trust. The interest of a beneficiary entitled to the remaining part of a trust will be equal to 100 per cent less the aggregate percentages held by income beneficiaries. A beneficiary's interest in a trust will not be considered to be owned by a person entitled to benefits under the other provisions of paragraph 2 if it is not possible to determine the beneficiary's actuarial interest. Consequently, if it is not possible to determine the actuarial interest of the beneficiaries in a trust, the ownership test under subdivision i) cannot be satisfied, unless all possible beneficiaries are persons entitled to benefits under the other subparagraphs of paragraph 2.

28. Subdivision ii), which constitutes the base erosion part of the test, is satisfied with respect to a person if less than 50 per cent of the person's gross income for the taxable period, as determined under the tax law in the person's State of residence, is paid or accrued to persons who are not residents of either Contracting State entitled to benefits under subparagraphs a), b) or d), or subdivision i) of subparagraph c), in the form of payments deductible for tax purposes in the payer's State of residence.

29. For the purposes of the test in subdivision ii), deductible (i.e. base-eroding) payments do not include arm's-length payments in the ordinary course of business for services or tangible property. To the extent they are deductible from the taxable base under the tax law in the person's State of residence, trust distributions constitute such base-eroding payments. Depreciation and amortisation deductions, which do not represent payments or accruals to other persons, are not taken into account for the purposes of subdivision ii). Income that is subjected to full taxation in the State of source should not be considered to be a base-eroding payment even if it is deductible by the payer. For example, the payment of a "group contribution" that may be made by a company that is a resident of a Contracting State to the permanent establishment, situated in the same State, of a non-resident company that is part of the same group should not be taken into account as such a payment would be taxable in the same State where it would be deducted.

30. ***The ownership and base erosion tests included in subparagraph e) require a determination for each taxable period of the entity; when these tests are met for a given taxable period, the entity constitutes a qualified person at any time within that taxable period. The taxable period to which subparagraph e) refers is determined by the taxation law of the State of residence of the entity.***

Collective investment vehicles – subparagraph 2 f)

<u>*Detailed version*</u>

<u>*f)*</u> <u>[*possible provision on collective investment vehicles*]</u>[1]

<u>*[Footnote 1] This subparagraph should be drafted (or omitted) based on how collective investment vehicles are treated in the Convention and are used and treated in each Contracting State: see the Commentary on the subparagraph and paragraphs 6.4 to 6.38 of the Commentary on Article 1.*</u>

Commentary on the detailed version

31. ***As indicated in the footnote to subparagraph f), whether a specific rule concerning collective investment vehicles (CIVs) should be included in paragraph 2, and, if so, how that rule should be drafted, will depend on how the Convention applies to CIVs and on the treatment and use of CIVs in each Contracting State. Such a specific rule will frequently be needed since a CIV may not be a qualified person under either the other provisions of paragraph 2 or 3, because, in many cases***

- ***the interests in the CIV are not publicly-traded (even though these interests are widely distributed);***
- ***these interests are held by residents of third States;***
- ***the distributions made by the CIV are deductible payments, and***
- ***the CIV is used for investment purposes rather than for the "active conduct of a business" within the meaning of paragraph 3.***

32. ***Paragraphs 6.8 to 6.34 of the Commentary on Article 1 discuss various factors that should be considered for the purpose of determining the treaty entitlement of CIVs and these paragraphs are therefore relevant when determining whether a provision on CIVs should be included in paragraph 2 and how it should be drafted. These paragraphs include alternative provisions that may be used to deal adequately with the CIVs that are found in each Contracting State. As explained below, the use of these provisions may make it unnecessary to include a specific rule on CIVs in paragraph 2, although it will be important to make sure that, in such a case, the definition of "equivalent beneficiary", if the term is used for the purposes of one of these alternative provisions, is adapted to reflect the definition included in paragraph 6.***

33. ***If it is included, subparagraph f) will address cases where a Contracting State agrees that CIVs established in the other Contracting State constitute residents of that other State under the analysis in paragraphs 6.9 to 6.12 of the Commentary on Article 1 (such agreement may be evidenced by a mutual agreement as envisaged in paragraph 6.16 of the Commentary on Article 1 or may result from judicial or administrative pronouncements). The provisions of***

the Article, including subparagraph f), are not relevant with respect to a CIV that does not qualify as a resident of a Contracting State under the analysis in paragraphs 6.9 to 6.12 of the Commentary on Article 1. Also, the provisions of subparagraph f) are not relevant where the treaty entitlement of a CIV is dealt with under a treaty provision similar to one of the alternative provisions in paragraphs 6.17, 6.21, 6.26, 6.27 and 6.32 of the Commentary on Article 1.

34. As explained in paragraphs 6.19 and 6.20 of the Commentary on Article 1, Contracting States wishing to address the issue of CIVs' entitlement to treaty benefits may want to consider the economic characteristics, including the potential for treaty shopping, of the different types of CIVs that are used in each Contracting State.

35. As a result of that analysis, they may conclude that the tax treatment of CIVs established in the two States does not give rise to treaty-shopping concerns and decide to include in their bilateral treaty the alternative provision in paragraph 6.17 of the Commentary on Article 1, which would expressly provide for the treaty entitlement of CIVs established in each State and, at the same time, would ensure that they constitute qualified persons under subparagraph a) of paragraph 2 of the Article (because a CIV to which that alternative provision would apply would be treated as an individual). In such a case, subparagraph f) should be omitted. States that share the view that CIVs established in the two States do not give rise to treaty shopping concerns but that do not include in their treaty the alternative provision in paragraph 6.17 of the Commentary on Article 1 should ensure that any CIV that is a resident of a Contracting State should constitute a qualified person. In that case, subparagraph f) should be drafted as follows:

> *f) a CIV [a definition of CIV would be included in subparagraph f) of paragraph 6];*

36. The Contracting States could, however, conclude that CIVs present the opportunity for residents of third States to receive treaty benefits that would not have been available if these residents had invested directly and, for that reason, might prefer to draft subparagraph f) in a way that will ensure that a CIV that is a resident of a Contracting State will constitute a qualified person but only to the extent that the beneficial interests in the CIV are owned by equivalent beneficiaries. In that case, subparagraph f) should be drafted as follows:

> *f) a collective investment vehicle, but only to the extent that, at that time, the beneficial interests in the CIV are owned by residents of the Contracting State in which the collective investment vehicle is established or by equivalent beneficiaries.*

37. That treatment corresponds to the treatment that would result from the inclusion in a tax treaty of a provision similar to the alternative provision in paragraph 6.21 of the Commentary on Article 1. As explained in paragraphs 6.18 to 6.24 of the Commentary on Article 1, the inclusion of such an alternative provision would provide a more comprehensive solution to treaty issues arising in connection with CIVs because it would address treaty-shopping concerns whilst, at the same time, clarifying the tax treaty treatment of CIVs in both Contracting States. If that alternative provision is included in a tax treaty, subparagraph f) would not be necessary as regards the CIVs to which that alternative provision would apply: since that alternative provision provides that a CIV to which it applies shall be treated as an individual (to the extent that the beneficial interests in that CIV are owned by equivalent beneficiaries), that CIV will constitute a qualified person under subparagraph a) of paragraph 2 of the Article.

38. The approach described in the preceding two paragraphs, like the approach in paragraphs 6.21, 6.26 and 6.28 of the Commentary on Article 1, makes it necessary for the CIV to make a determination, when a benefit is claimed as regards a specific item of income, regarding the proportion of holders of interests who would have been entitled to benefits had they invested directly. As indicated in paragraph 6.29 of the Commentary on Article 1, however, the ownership of interests in CIVs changes regularly, and such interests frequently are held through intermediaries. For that reason, the CIV and its managers often do not themselves know the names and treaty status of the beneficial owners of interests. It would therefore be impractical for the CIV to collect such information from the relevant intermediaries each time the CIV receives income. Accordingly, Contracting States should be willing to accept practical and reliable approaches that do not require such daily tracing. As indicated in paragraph 6.31 of the Commentary on Article 1, the proportion of investors in the CIV is likely to change relatively slowly even though the identity of individual investors will change daily. For that reason, the determination of the extent to which the beneficial interests in a CIV are owned by equivalent beneficiaries should be made at regular intervals, the determination made at a given time being applicable to payments received until the following determination. This corresponds to the approach described in paragraph 6.31 of the Commentary on Article 1, according to which:

> *… it would be a reasonable approach to require the CIV to collect from other intermediaries, on specified dates, information enabling the CIV to determine the proportion of investors that are treaty-entitled. This information could be required at the end of a calendar or fiscal year or, if market conditions suggest that turnover in ownership is high, it could be required more frequently, although no more often than the end of each calendar quarter. The CIV could then make a claim on the basis of an average of those amounts over an agreed-upon time period. In adopting such procedures, care would have to be taken in choosing the measurement dates to ensure that the CIV would have enough time to update the information that it provides to other payers so that the correct amount is withheld at the beginning of each relevant period.*

39. Another view that Contracting States may adopt regarding CIVs is that expressed in paragraph 6.26 of the Commentary on Article 1. Contracting States that adopt that view may wish to draft subparagraph f) so that a CIV that is a resident of a Contracting State would only constitute a qualified person to the extent that the beneficial interests in that CIV are owned by residents of the Contracting State in which the CIV is established. In that case, subparagraph f) should be drafted as follows:

> *f) a collective investment vehicle, but only to the extent that, at that time, the beneficial interests in the collective investment vehicle are owned by residents of the Contracting State in which the collective investment vehicle is established.*

Since the inclusion of the alternative provision in paragraph 6.26 of the Commentary on Article 1 would achieve the same result with respect to the CIVs to which it would apply, subparagraph f) would not be necessary, if that alternative provision is included in a treaty, as regards the CIVs to which that provision would apply.

40. A variation on the preceding approach would be to consider that a CIV that is a resident of a Contracting State should constitute a qualified person if the majority of the beneficial interests in that CIV are owned by individuals who are residents of the Contracting State in which the CIV is established. This result could be achieved by omitting subparagraph f) and simply relying on the application of subparagraph 2) e) (the so-called ownership and base erosion test).

41. Another possible view that the Contracting States could adopt would be to conclude that the fact that a substantial proportion of the CIV's investors are treaty-eligible is adequate protection against treaty shopping, and thus that it is appropriate to provide an ownership threshold above which benefits would be provided with respect to all income received by a CIV. An alternative provision that would ensure that result is included in paragraph 6.27 of the Commentary on Article 1 and subparagraph f) would not be necessary, if the Contracting States include that provision in their bilateral treaty, with respect to the CIVs to which the provision would apply. If that provision is not included in the treaty, the scope of subparagraph f) could be broadened in order to achieve a similar result by referring to "a collective investment vehicle, but only if [ ] per cent of the beneficial interests in the collective investment vehicle are owned by residents of the Contracting State in which the collective investment vehicle is established and equivalent beneficiaries".

42. Similarly, the Contracting States may use the alternative provision in paragraph 6.32 of the Commentary on Article 1 where they consider "that a publicly-traded collective investment vehicle cannot be used effectively for treaty shopping because the shareholders or unit holders of such a collective investment vehicle cannot individually exercise control over it". In such case, subparagraph f) would not be necessary with respect to the CIVs to which the alternative provision would apply. States that share that view but that have not included the alternative provision in their treaty could draft subparagraph f) to read:

> *f) a collective investment vehicle if the principal class of shares in the collective investment vehicle is listed and regularly traded on a recognised stock exchange.*

43. Finally, as explained in paragraph 6.25 of the Commentary on Article 1, States that share the concern described in that paragraph about the potential deferral of taxation that could arise with respect to a CIV that is subject to no or low taxation and that may accumulate its income rather than distributing it on a current basis may wish to negotiate provisions that extend benefits only to those CIVs that are required to distribute earnings currently. Depending on their drafting, such provisions may render subparagraph f) unnecessary.

Active conduct of a business

Simplified version

4. a) A resident of a Contracting State that is neither a qualified person nor entitled under paragraph 3 to a benefit that would otherwise be accorded by this Convention with respect to an item of income shall nevertheless be entitled to such benefit if the resident is carrying on a business in the first-mentioned Contracting State (other than the business of making or managing investments for the resident's own account, unless the business is carried on by a bank, an insurance company, a registered securities dealer or any other institution agreed upon by the Contracting States) and that item of income is derived in connection with, or is incidental to, that business.

b) If a resident of a Contracting State derives an item of income from a business carried on by that resident in the other Contracting State, or derives an item of income arising in the other Contracting State from a related enterprise of the resident, the conditions described in subparagraph a) shall be considered to be satisfied with respect to such item of income only if the business carried on by the resident in the first-mentioned Contracting State is substantial in relation to the business carried on by the resident or related enterprise in the other Contracting State. Whether a business is substantial for the purpose of this subparagraph shall be determined on the basis of all the facts and circumstances.

c) For the purposes of this paragraph, the business carried on by a partnership in which a person is a partner and the business carried on by related enterprises of a person shall be deemed to be carried on by such person.

Detailed version

3. a) A resident of a Contracting State will be entitled to benefits of this Convention with respect to an item of income derived from the other Contracting State, regardless of whether the resident is a qualified person, if the resident is engaged in the active conduct of a business in the first-mentioned Contracting State (other than the business of making or managing investments for the resident's own account, unless these activities are banking, insurance or securities activities carried on by a bank or [list financial institutions similar to banks that the Contracting States agree to treat as such], insurance enterprise or registered securities dealer respectively), and the income derived from the other Contracting State is derived in connection with, or is incidental to, that business.

b) If a resident of a Contracting State derives an item of income from a business activity conducted by that resident in the other Contracting State, or derives an item of income arising in the other Contracting State from an associated enterprise, the conditions described in subparagraph a) shall be considered to be satisfied with respect to such item only if the business activity carried on by the resident in the first-mentioned Contracting State is substantial in relation to the business activity carried on by the resident or associated enterprise in the other Contracting State. Whether a business activity is substantial for the purposes of this paragraph will be determined based on all the facts and circumstances.

c) For purposes of applying this paragraph, activities conducted by persons connected to a person shall be deemed to be conducted by such person. A person shall be connected to another if one possesses at least 50 per cent of the beneficial interest in the other (or, in the case of a company, at least 50 per cent of the aggregate vote and value of the company's shares or of the beneficial equity interest in the company) or another person possesses at least 50 per cent of the beneficial interest (or, in the case of a company, at least 50 per cent of the aggregate voting power and value of the company's shares or of the beneficial equity interest in the company) in each person. In any case, a person shall be considered to be connected to another if, based on all the relevant facts and circumstances, one has control of the other or both are under the control of the same person or persons.

Commentary on the detailed version

44. Paragraph 3 sets forth an alternative test under which a resident of a Contracting State may receive treaty benefits with respect to certain items of income that are connected to an active business conducted in its State of residence. This paragraph recognises that where an entity resident of a Contracting State actively carries on business activities in that State, including activities conducted by connected persons, and derives income from the other Contracting State in connection with, or incidental to, such business activities, granting treaty benefits with respect to such income does not give rise to treaty-shopping concerns regardless of the nature and ownership of the entity. The paragraph will provide treaty benefits in a large number of situations where benefits would otherwise be denied under paragraph 1 because the entity is not a "qualified person" under paragraph 2.

45. A resident of a Contracting State may qualify for benefits under paragraph 3 whether or not it also qualifies under paragraph 2. Under the active-conduct test of paragraph 3, a person (typically a company) will be eligible for treaty benefits if it satisfies two conditions: (1) it is engaged in the active conduct of a business in its State of residence; and (2) the payment for which benefits are sought is related to the business. In certain cases, an additional requirement that the business be substantial in size relative to the activity in the source State generating the income must be met.

46. Subparagraph a) sets forth the general rule that a resident of a Contracting State engaged in the active conduct of a business in that State may obtain the benefits of the Convention with respect to an item of income derived from the other Contracting State. The item of income, however, must be derived in connection with, or be incidental to, that business.

47. The term "business" is not defined and, under the general rule of paragraph 2 of Article 3, must therefore be given the meaning that it has under domestic law. An entity generally will be considered to be engaged in the active conduct of a business only if persons through whom the entity is acting (such as officers or employees of a company) conduct substantial managerial and operational activities.

48. The business of making or managing investments for the resident's own account will be considered to be a business only when the relevant activities are part of banking, insurance or securities activities conducted by a bank or financial institution that the Contracting States would consider to be similar to a bank (such as a credit union or building society), an insurance enterprise or a registered securities dealer respectively. Such activities conducted by a person other than a bank (or financial institution agreed to by the Contracting States), insurance enterprise or registered securities dealer will not be considered to be the active conduct of a business, nor would they be considered to be the active conduct of a business if conducted by a bank (or financial institution agreed to by the Contracting States), insurance enterprise or registered securities dealer but not as part of the enterprise's banking, insurance or dealer business. Since a headquarters operation is in the business of managing investments, a company that functions solely as a headquarters company will not be considered to be engaged in the active conduct of a business for purposes of paragraph 3.

49. An item of income is derived in connection with a business if the income-producing activity in the State of source is a line of business that "forms a part of" or is "complementary to" the business conducted in the State of residence by the income recipient.

50. A business activity generally will be considered to form part of a business activity conducted in the State of source if the two activities involve the design, manufacture or sale of the same products or type of products, or the provision of similar services. The line of business in the State of residence may be upstream, downstream, or parallel to the activity conducted in the State of source. Thus, the line of business may provide inputs for a manufacturing process that occurs in the State of source, may sell the output of that manufacturing process, or simply may sell the same sorts of products that are being sold by the business carried on in the State of source. The following examples illustrate these principles:

- *Example 1: ACO is a company resident of State A and is engaged in an active manufacturing business in that State. ACO owns 100 per cent of the shares of BCO, a company resident of State B. BCO distributes ACO's products in State B. Since the business activities conducted by the two companies involve the same products, BCO's distribution business is considered to form a part of ACO's manufacturing business.*
- *Example 2: The facts are the same as in Example 1, except that ACO does not manufacture products. Rather, ACO operates a large research and development facility in State A that licenses intellectual property to affiliates worldwide, including BCO. BCO and other affiliates then manufacture and market the ACO-designed products in their respective markets. Since the activities conducted by ACO and BCO involve the same product lines, these activities are considered to form a part of the same business.*

51. For two activities to be considered to be "complementary," the activities need not relate to the same types of products or services, but they should be part of the same overall industry and be related in the sense that the success or failure of one activity will tend to result in success or failure for the other.

Where more than one business is conducted in the State of source and only one of the businesses forms a part of or is complementary to a business conducted in the State of residence, it is necessary to identify the business to which an item of income is attributable. Royalties generally will be considered to be derived in connection with the business to which the underlying intangible property is attributable. Dividends will be deemed to be derived first out of profits of the treaty-benefited business, and then out of other profits. Interest income may be allocated under any reasonable method consistently applied.

- *Example 3. CCO is a company resident of State C that operates an international airline. DCO is a wholly-owned subsidiary of CCO resident of State D. DCO operates a chain of hotels in State D that are located near airports served by flights operated by CCO. CCO frequently sells tour packages that include air travel to State D and lodging at DCO's hotels. Although both companies are engaged in the active conduct of a business, the businesses of operating a chain of hotels and operating an airline are distinct businesses. Therefore DCO's business does not form a part of CCO's business. DCO's business, however, is considered to be complementary to CCO's business because these two businesses are part of the same overall industry (travel) and the links between these activities tend to make them interdependent.*
- *Example 4. The facts are the same as in Example 3, except that DCO owns an office building in the other Contracting State instead of a hotel chain. No part of CCO's business is conducted through the office building. DCO's business is not considered to form a part of or to be complementary to CCO's business. They are engaged in distinct businesses in separate industries, and there is no economic dependence between the two operations.*
- *Example 5. ECO is a company resident of State E. ECO produces and sells flowers in State E and other countries. ECO owns all the shares of FCO, a company resident of State F. FCO is a holding company that is not engaged in a business. FCO owns all the shares of three companies that are resident of State F: GCO, HCO and ICO. GCO distributes ECO's flowers under the ECO trademark in State F. HCO markets a line of lawn care products in State F under the ECO trademark. In addition to being sold under the same trademark, GCO's and HCO's products are sold in the same stores and sales of each company's products tend to generate increased sales of the other's products. ICO imports fish from State E and distributes it to fish wholesalers in State F. For purposes of paragraph 3, the business of GCO forms a part of the business of ECO, the business of HCO is complementary to the business of ECO, and the business of ICO is neither part of nor complementary to that of ECO.*
- *Example 6. JCO is a company resident of State J. JCO produces and sells baby food in State J and other countries. JCO acquires all the shares of KCO, a company resident of State K that produces and distributes jam and similar food products. JCO and KCO are both involved in the food industry, the products resulting from the businesses activities carried on by these companies are sold in the same stores and sales of*

> ***each company's products would be affected by any incident related to the quality of any of their products. For purposes of paragraph 3, the business of KCO is complementary to the business of JCO.***

52. An item of income derived from the State of source is "incidental to" the business carried on in the State of residence if production of the item facilitates the conduct of the business in the State of residence. An example of incidental income is income derived from the temporary investment of working capital of a resident of one Contracting State.

53. Subparagraph b) of paragraph 3 states a further condition to the general rule in subparagraph a) in cases where the business generating the item of income in question is carried on either by the person deriving the income or by any associated enterprises. Subparagraph b) states that the business carried on in the State of residence, under these circumstances, must be substantial in relation to the activity in the State of source. The substantiality requirement is intended to prevent a narrow case of treaty-shopping abuses in which a company attempts to qualify for benefits by engaging in de minimis connected business activities in the treaty State of which it is resident (i.e. activities that have little economic cost or effect with respect to the company's business as a whole).

54. The determination of substantiality is made based upon all the facts and circumstances and takes into account the comparative sizes of the businesses in each Contracting State, the nature of the activities performed in each Contracting State, and the relative contributions made to that business in each Contracting State. In any case, in making each determination or comparison, due regard will be given to the relative sizes of the economies and the markets in the two Contracting States.

- ***Example 7. LCO is a pharmaceutical company resident of State L. LCO is engaged in an active manufacturing business in State L and also conducts research and development in State L. All the shares of LCO are owned by OCO, a company resident of State O. LCO has developed different anti-malaria drugs which are produced, under LCO's patents and trademarks, by MCO, a subsidiary of LCO which is a resident of State M. LCO sells these drugs, along with the other drugs that it manufactures, in State L and other States where malaria is almost non-existent. MCO pays a royalty to LCO for the use of the IP. Taking into account the nature of the business activities performed in State L and State M and the relative contribution made to the trade or business in each state, the royalty payment is entitled to treaty benefits. Due regard is also given to the relative small size of the market of anti-malaria drugs in State L (where the drugs are primarily sold to people who travel to parts of the world where malaria is widespread) compared to the market for such products in State M. Given the nature of the market for the drug in each country as well as all the other facts and circumstances, the business activity carried on by LCO in State L may be considered substantial in relation to the business activity carried on by MCO in State M.***
- ***Example 8: PCO, a company resident of State P, a developing country, has developed a line of luxury cosmetics that incorporate ingredients from plants that are primarily found in State P. PCO is***

the owner of patents, trade names and trademarks for these cosmetics. PCO's shares are held in equal proportion by three shareholders: a company that is a resident of State P, another company that is a resident of State Q and a third company that is a resident of State R. PCO harvests and conditions the plants in State P. The plants are then shipped to State S (a large affluent country where there is an important demand for luxury cosmetics) where they are transformed into cosmetics by SCO, a subsidiary of PCO that is a resident of State S. The cosmetics are distributed in State S by another subsidiary, TCO, which is also a resident of State S, under trade names and trademarks licensed to TCO by PCO. The cosmetics are labelled "made in State S". Due to the relatively small size of the economy of State P compared to the size of the economy of State S, the business activity carried on by PCO in State P is substantial in relation to the business activity carried on by SCO and TCO in State S.

55. The determination in subparagraph b) also is made separately for each item of income derived from the State of source. It is therefore possible that a person would be entitled to the benefits of the Convention with respect to one item of income but not with respect to another. If a resident of a Contracting State is entitled to treaty benefits with respect to a particular item of income under paragraph 3, the resident is entitled to all benefits of the Convention insofar as they affect the taxation of that item of income in the State of source.

56. The application of the substantiality requirement only to income from associated enterprises focuses only on potential abuse cases, and does not hamper certain other kinds of non-abusive activities, even though the income recipient resident in a Contracting State may be very small in relation to the entity generating income in the other Contracting State. For example, if a small research firm in one State develops a process that it licenses to a very large, unrelated, pharmaceutical manufacturer in another State, the size of the research firm in the first State would not have to be tested against the size of the manufacturer. Similarly, a small bank of one State that makes a loan to a very large unrelated company operating a business in the other State would not have to pass a substantiality test to receive treaty benefits under paragraph 3.

57. Subparagraph c) of paragraph 3 provides special attribution rules for purposes of applying the substantive rules of subparagraphs a) and b). Thus, these rules apply for purposes of determining whether a person meets the requirements in subparagraph a) that it be engaged in the active conduct of a business and that the item of income is derived in connection with that active business, and for making the comparison required by the "substantiality" requirement in subparagraph b). Subparagraph c) attributes to a person activities conducted by persons "connected" to such person. A person ("X") is connected to another person ("Y") if X possesses 50 per cent or more of the beneficial interest in Y (or if Y possesses 50 per cent or more of the beneficial interest in X). For this purpose, X is connected to a company if X owns shares representing 50 per cent or more of the aggregate voting power and value of the company or 50 per cent or more of the beneficial equity interest in the company. X also is connected to Y if a third person possesses 50 per cent or more of the beneficial interest in both X and Y. For this purpose, if X or Y is a company, the threshold relationship with respect to such company or companies is 50 per cent or more of the aggregate voting power and value or 50 per cent or more of the beneficial equity interest. Finally, X is connected to Y if, based upon all the facts and circumstances, X controls Y, Y controls X, or X and Y are controlled by the same person or persons.

Derivative benefits

Simplified version

3. A resident of a Contracting State that is not a qualified person shall nevertheless be entitled to a benefit that would otherwise be accorded by this Convention with respect to an item of income if persons that are equivalent beneficiaries own, directly or indirectly, more than 75 per cent of the beneficial interests of the resident.

Detailed version

[4. A company that is a resident of a Contracting State shall also be entitled to a benefit that would otherwise be accorded by this Convention if, at the time when that benefit would be accorded:

a) at least 95 per cent of the aggregate voting power and value of its shares (and at least 50 percent of any disproportionate class of shares) is owned, directly or indirectly, by seven or fewer persons that are equivalent beneficiaries, provided that in the case of indirect ownership, each intermediate owner is itself an equivalent beneficiary, and

b) less than 50 per cent of the company's gross income, as determined in the company's State of residence, for the taxable period that includes that time, is paid or accrued, directly or indirectly, to persons who are not equivalent beneficiaries, in the form of payments (but not including arm's length payments in the ordinary course of business for services or tangible property) that are deductible for the purposes of the taxes covered by this Convention in the company's State of residence.][11]

Commentary on the detailed version

58. Paragraph 4 sets forth a derivative benefits test that is potentially applicable to all treaty benefits, although the test is applied to individual items of income. In general, this derivative benefits test entitles certain companies that are residents of a Contracting State to treaty benefits if the owner of the company would have been entitled to at least the same benefit had the income in question flowed directly to that owner. To qualify under this paragraph, the company must meet an ownership test and a base erosion test.

59. Subparagraph a) sets forth the ownership test. Under this test, seven or fewer equivalent beneficiaries must own shares representing at least 95 per cent of the aggregate voting power and value of the company and at least 50 per cent of any disproportionate class of shares. Ownership may be direct or indirect. The term "equivalent beneficiary" is defined in subparagraph f) of paragraph 6.

60. Subparagraph b) sets forth the base erosion test. A company meets this base erosion test if less than 50 percent of its gross income (as determined in the company's State of residence) for the taxable period that includes the time when the benefit would be accorded is paid or accrued, directly or indirectly, to a person or persons who are not equivalent beneficiaries in the form of payments deductible for tax purposes in the company's State of residence. These amounts do not include arm's length payments in the ordinary course of business for services or tangible property. This test is the same as the base erosion test in subparagraph e) (ii) of paragraph 2, except that the test in subparagraph b) focuses on base eroding payments to persons who are not equivalent beneficiaries.

61. Some States consider that the provisions of paragraph 4 create unacceptable risks of treaty shopping with respect to payments that are deductible in the State of source. These States prefer to restrict the scope of paragraph 4 to dividends, which are typically not deductible. States that share that view are free to amend the first part of the paragraph so that it reads as follows:

> *4. A company that is a resident of a Contracting State shall also be entitled to a benefit that would otherwise be accorded under Article 10 of this Convention if, at the time when that benefit would be accorded:*

Discretionary relief

Simplified version

5. A resident of a Contracting State that is neither a qualified person nor entitled under paragraph 3 or 4 to a benefit that would otherwise be accorded by this Convention with respect to an item of income shall nevertheless be entitled to such benefit if the competent authority of the Contracting State from which the benefit is being claimed, upon request from that resident, determines, in accordance with its domestic law or administrative practice, that the establishment, acquisition or maintenance of the resident and the conduct of its operations are considered as not having as one of its principal purposes the obtaining of such benefit. The competent authority of the Contracting State to which such request has been made by a resident of the other Contracting State shall consult with the competent authority of that other State before rejecting the request.

Detailed version

5. If a resident of a Contracting State is not entitled, under the preceding provisions of this Article, to all benefits provided under this Convention, the competent authority of the Contracting State that would otherwise have granted benefits to which that resident is not entitled shall nevertheless treat that resident as being entitled to these benefits, or benefits with respect to a specific item of income or capital, if such competent authority, upon request from that resident and after consideration of the relevant facts and circumstances, determines that the establishment, acquisition or maintenance of the resident and the conduct of its operations did not have as one of its principal purposes the obtaining of benefits under this Convention. The competent authority of the Contracting State to which the request has been made will consult with the competent authority of the other State before rejecting a request made under this paragraph by a resident of that other State.

Commentary on the detailed version

62. Paragraph 5 provides that where, under paragraphs 1 to 4 of the Article, a resident of one of the Contracting States is not entitled to all benefits of the

Convention in a Contracting State, that resident may request the competent authority of that State to grant these benefits. In such a case, the competent authority will grant these benefits if, after considering the relevant facts and circumstances, it determines that neither the establishment, acquisition, or maintenance of the resident, nor the conduct of its operations, had as one of its principal purposes the obtaining of benefits under the Convention.

63. Through this paragraph, a resident that is not entitled to the benefits of the Convention under paragraphs 1 through 4 but who has a substantial relationship to its State of residence, taking into account considerations in addition to those addressed through the objective tests in paragraphs 1 through 4, may be able to obtain treaty benefits where the allowance of benefits would not otherwise be contrary to the purposes of the Convention. In the case of a resident subsidiary company with a parent in a third State, whilst the fact that the relevant withholding rate provided in the Convention is not lower than the corresponding withholding rate in the tax treaty between the State of source and the third State would be a relevant factor, that fact would not, in itself, be sufficient to establish that the conditions for granting the discretionary relief are met. Similarly, where a foreign company is engaged in a mobile business such as financing, or where the domestic law of a Contracting State provides a special tax treatment for certain activities conducted in special zones or offshore (e.g. licensing intangibles) those factors will not be evidence of a non-tax business reason for locating in that State. In such cases, additional favourable business factors must be present to establish a substantial relationship to that State. Paragraph 5 also provides that the competent authority of the State to which the request is made will consult with the competent authority of the other State before refusing to exercise its discretion to grant benefits to a resident of that other State.

64. In order to be granted benefits under paragraph 5, the person must establish, to the satisfaction of the competent authority of the State from which benefits are being sought, that there were clear non-tax business reasons for its formation, acquisition, or maintenance and for the conduct of its operation in the other Contracting State. What the purposes are for the establishment, acquisition or maintenance of a person and the conduct of its operations are questions of fact which can only be answered by considering all relevant circumstances on a case by case basis. It is not necessary to find conclusive proof of intent, but the competent authority must be able to conclude, after an objective analysis of the relevant facts and circumstances, that none of the principal purposes for the establishment, acquisition or maintenance of the person and the conduct of its operations was to obtain benefits under the Convention. Whilst it should not be lightly assumed that obtaining benefits under a convention was one of these principal purposes, a person should not expect to obtain relief under paragraph 5 by merely asserting that its establishment, acquisition or maintenance and the conduct of its operations were not undertaken to obtain the benefits of the Convention. All of the evidence must be provided to the competent authority in order to enable it to determine whether this is the case.

65. The reference to "one of the principal purposes" in paragraph 5 means that obtaining benefits under a tax treaty need not be the sole or dominant purpose for the establishment, acquisition or maintenance of the person and the conduct of its operations. It is sufficient that at least one of the principal purposes was to obtain treaty benefits. Where the competent authority determines, having regard to all relevant facts and circumstances, that obtaining benefits under the Convention was not a principal consideration and would not have justified the establishment, acquisition or maintenance of the person and the conduct of its operations, it shall treat that person as being entitled to these benefits, or benefits with respect to a specific item of income or capital. Where, however, the establishment, acquisition or maintenance of the person and the conduct of its operations is carried on for the purpose of obtaining similar benefits under a number of treaties, it should not be considered that obtaining benefits under other treaties will prevent the obtaining of benefits under one treaty from being considered a principal purpose for these operations.

65.1 The competent authority that receives a request for relief under paragraph 5 should process that request expeditiously.

66. Although such a request will usually be made by a resident of a Contracting State to the competent authority of the other Contracting State, there may be cases in which a resident of a Contracting State may request the competent authority of its own State of residence to grant relief under paragraph 5. This would be the case if the treaty benefits that are requested are provided by the State of residence, such as the benefits of the provisions of Articles 23 A and 23 B concerning the elimination of double taxation. In such cases, the paragraph does not require the competent authority to consult the competent authority of the other State before denying the request.

67. The paragraph grants broad discretion to the competent authority and, as long as the competent authority has exercised that discretion in accordance with the requirements of the paragraph, it cannot be considered that the decision of the competent authority is an action that results in taxation not in accordance with the provisions of the Convention (see paragraph 1 of Article 25). The paragraph does require, however, that the competent authority must consider the relevant facts and circumstances before reaching a decision and must consult the competent authority of the other Contracting State before rejecting a request to grant benefits. The first requirement seeks to ensure that the competent authority will consider each request on its own merits whilst the requirement that the competent authority of the other Contracting State be consulted should ensure that Contracting States treat similar cases in a consistent manner and can justify their decision on the basis of the facts and circumstances of the particular case. This consultation process does not, however, require that the competent authority to which the request has been presented obtain the agreement of the competent authority that is consulted. The determination that neither the establishment, acquisition or maintenance of the resident making the request, nor the conduct of its operations, had as one of its principal purposes the obtaining of benefits under the Convention is a matter that is left to the discretion of the competent authority to which the request is made. Once it has determined that this is the case, the competent authority is required to grant benefits but it may then grant all of the benefits of the Convention to the taxpayer making the request, or it may grant only certain benefits. For instance, it may grant benefits only with respect to a particular item of income in a manner similar to paragraph 3. Further, the competent authority may establish conditions, such as setting time limits on the duration of any relief granted.

68. The request for a determination under paragraph 5 may be presented before (e.g. through a ruling request) or after the establishment, acquisition or maintenance of the person for whom the request is made. Where the request is made after such establishment, acquisition or maintenance, any benefits granted by the competent authority may be allowed retroactively.

69. Whilst it is impossible to provide a detailed list of all the facts and circumstances that would be relevant to the determination referred to in paragraph 5, examples of such facts and circumstances include the history, structure, ownership and operations of the resident that makes the request, whether that resident is a long standing entity that was recently acquired by non-residents for non-tax reasons, whether the resident carries on substantial business activities, whether the resident's income for which the benefits are requested is subject to double taxation and whether the establishment or use of the resident gives rise to non-taxation or reduced taxation of the income.

69.1 To reduce the resource implications of having to consider requests for discretionary relief, and to discourage vexatious requests, Contracting States may find it useful to publish guidelines on the types of cases that it considers will and will not qualify for discretionary relief. However, any administrative conditions that a Contracting State imposes on applicants should not deter persons making requests where they consider that they have a reasonable prospect of satisfying a competent authority that benefits should be granted.

Definitions

Simplified version

6. For the purposes of this Article:

Detailed version

6. For purposes of the preceding provisions of this Article:

69.2 Paragraph 6 includes a number of definitions that apply for the purposes of the Article. These definitions supplement the definitions included in Articles 3, 4 and 5 of the Convention, which apply throughout the Convention.

The term "recognised stock exchange"

Simplified version

b) the term "recognised stock exchange" means:

i) any stock exchange established and regulated as such under the laws of either Contracting State; and

ii) any other stock exchange agreed upon by the competent authorities of the Contracting States;

Detailed version

a) the term "recognised stock exchange" means:

i) [list of stock exchanges agreed to at the time of signature]; and

ii) any other stock exchange agreed upon by the competent authorities of the Contracting States;

Commentary on the detailed version

70. The definition of "recognised stock exchange" first includes stock exchanges that both Contracting States agree to identify at the time of the signature of the Convention. Although this would typically include stock exchanges established in the Contracting States on which shares of publicly listed companies and entities that are residents of these States are actively traded, the stock exchanges to be identified in the definition need not be established in one of the Contracting States. This recognises that the globalisation of financial markets and the prominence of some large financial centres have resulted in the shares of many public companies being actively traded on more than one stock exchange and on stock exchanges situated outside the State of residence of these companies.

71. The definition also allows the competent authorities of the Contracting States to supplement, through a subsequent agreement, the list of stock exchanges identified in the definition at the time of signature of the Convention.

71.1 The stock exchanges to be included in the definition should impose listing requirements that ensure that shares of entities listed on that stock exchange are genuinely publicly traded. The following factors should be considered when determining whether a stock exchange should be listed in the definition or subsequently added to that list through the competent authority agreement referred to in the preceding paragraph:

- *What are the requirements/standards with respect to listing a company on the stock exchange?*
- *What are the requirements/standards in order to continue to be listed on the stock exchange, including minimum financial standards?*
- *What are the annual/interim disclosure and/or filing requirements for companies whose shares are traded on the stock exchange?*
- *What is the volume of shares traded on the stock exchange in a calendar year?*
- *Do the rules governing the stock exchange ensure active trading of listed stocks? If so, how?*
- *Are the companies listed on the stock exchange required to disclose on an ongoing basis financial information and information on events that may have a material impact on their financial situations?*
- *Is information on the trading volume and overall shareholding of the companies listed on the stock exchange publicly available?*
- *Does the stock exchange impose any minimum size requirements, such as minimum capitalisation or number of employees, for companies whose shares are traded on the exchange?*
- *Does the stock exchange impose a required minimum percentage of public ownership? If so, what is the minimum amount?*
- *For a company to trade on the stock exchange, are the shares of companies required to be freely negotiable and fully paid for?*
- *Is the stock exchange required to disclose the share prices of its listed companies within a certain timeframe?*

- *Is the stock exchange regulated or supervised by a government authority of the country in which it is located?*
- *[In the case of a new stock exchange to be added to an existing list:] Why would a company prefer to list on the new exchange rather than on another exchange, including those exchanges that are already "recognised stock exchanges" in the tax treaty? For example, are there lesser corporate governance and financial disclosure requirements?*
- *[In the case of a new stock exchange to be added to an existing list:] Does the new stock exchange provide a more efficient vehicle for raising capital and, if so, why?*

The term "principal class of shares"

Simplified version

a) the term "principal class of shares" means the class or classes of shares of a company which represents in the aggregate a majority of the voting power of the company;

Detailed version

b) the term "principal class of shares" means the ordinary or common shares of the company, provided that such class of shares represents the majority of the voting power and value of the company. If no single class of ordinary or common shares represents the majority of the aggregate voting power and value of the company, the "principal class of shares" are those classes that in the aggregate represent a majority of the aggregate voting power and value of the company. In the case of a company participating in a dual listed company arrangement, the principal class of shares will be determined after excluding the special voting shares which were issued as a means of establishing that dual listed company arrangement.

Commentary on the detailed version

72. The definition of the term "principal class of shares" refers to the ordinary or common shares of a company but only if these shares represent the majority of the voting rights as well as of the value of the company. If a company has only one class of shares, it will naturally constitute its "principal class of shares". If a company has more than one class of shares, it is necessary to determine which class or classes constitute the "principal class of shares", which will be the class of shares, or any combination of classes of shares, that represent, in the aggregate, a majority of the voting power and value of the company. Although in a particular case involving a company with several classes of shares it is conceivable that more than one group of classes could be identified that would represent the majority of the voting power and value of the company, it is only necessary to identify one such group that meets the conditions of subparagraph c) of paragraph 2 in order for the company to be entitled to treaty benefits under that provision (benefits will not be denied to the company even if a second group of shares representing the majority of the voting power and value of the company, but not satisfying the conditions of subparagraph c) of paragraph 2, could be identified).

73. The last part of the definition provides an exception applicable to companies that participate in a dual listed company arrangement, as defined in paragraph g). In the case of these companies, special voting shares issued for the purposes of implementing that dual listed company arrangement must not be taken into account for the purposes of determining the principal class of shares of these companies.

The term "disproportionate class of shares"

Detailed version only

c) the term "disproportionate class of shares" means any class of shares of a company resident in one of the Contracting States that entitles the shareholder to disproportionately higher participation, through dividends, redemption payments or otherwise, in the earnings generated in the other Contracting State by particular assets or activities of the company;

74. Under the definition of the term "disproportionate class of shares", which is relevant for the purposes of paragraph 4 and subparagraphs c) and e) of paragraph 2, a company has a disproportionate class of shares if it has outstanding shares that are subject to terms or other arrangements that entitle the holder of these shares to a larger portion of the company's income derived from the other Contracting State than that to which the holder would be entitled in the absence of such terms or arrangements. Thus, for example, a company resident in one Contracting State has a "disproportionate class of shares" if some of the outstanding shares of that company are "tracking shares" that pay dividends based upon a formula that approximates the company's return on its assets employed in the other Contracting State. This is illustrated by the following example:

- *Example: ACO is a company resident of State A. ACO has issued common shares and preferred shares. The common shares are listed and regularly traded on the principal stock exchange of State A. The preferred shares have no voting rights and entitle their holders to receive dividends equal in amount to interest payments that ACO receives from unrelated borrowers in State B. The preferred shares are owned entirely by a single shareholder who is a resident of a third State with which State B does not have a tax treaty. The common shares account for more than 50 per cent of the value of ACO and for 100 per cent of the voting power. Since the owner of the preferred shares is entitled to receive payments corresponding to ACO's interest income arising in State B, the preferred shares constitute a "disproportionate class of shares" and because these shares are not regularly traded on a recognised stock exchange, ACO will not qualify for benefits under subparagraph c) of paragraph 2.*

The term "primary place of management and control"

Detailed version only

d) a company's "primary place of management and control" will be in the Contracting State of which it is a resident only if executive officers and senior management employees exercise day-to-day responsibility for more of the strategic, financial and operational policy decision making for the company (including its direct and indirect subsidiaries) in that Contracting State than in any other State and the staff of such persons conduct more of the day-to-day activities necessary for preparing and making those decisions in that Contracting State than in any other State;

75. The term "primary place of management and control" is relevant for the purposes of subparagraph c) of paragraph 2. This term must be distinguished from the concept of "place of effective management", which was used, before [date of the next update], in paragraph 3 of Article 4 and in various provisions, including Article 8, applicable to the operation of ships and aircraft. The concept of "place of effective management" was interpreted by some States as being ordinarily the place where the most senior person or group of persons (for example a board of directors) made the key management and commercial decisions necessary for the conduct of the company's business. The concept of the primary place of management and control, by contrast, refers to the place where the day-to-day responsibility for the management of the company (and its subsidiaries) is exercised. A company's primary place of management and control will be situated in the State of residence of that company only if the executive officers and senior management employees exercise day-to-day responsibility for more of the strategic, financial and operational policy decision making for the company (including direct and indirect subsidiaries) in that State than in the other State or any third State, and the staff that support the management in making those decisions are also based in that State. Thus, the test looks to the overall activities of the relevant persons to see where those activities are conducted. In most cases, it will be a necessary, but not a sufficient, condition that the headquarters of the company (that is, the place at which the chief executive officer and other top-level executives normally are based) be located in the Contracting State of which the company is a resident.

76. In order to determine a company's primary place of management and control, it is necessary to determine which persons are to be considered "executive officers and senior management employees". In some countries, it will not be necessary to look beyond the executives who are members of the board of directors (i.e. the so-called "inside directors"). That will not always be the case, however; in fact, the relevant persons may be employees of subsidiaries if those persons make the strategic, financial and operational policy decisions. Moreover, it would be necessary to take into account any special voting arrangements that result in certain persons making certain decisions without the participation of other persons.

The term "collective investment vehicle"

Detailed version only

e) [possible definition of "collective investment vehicle"];[1]

[***Footnote 1: A definition of the term "collective investment vehicle" should be added if a provision on collective investment vehicles is included in paragraph 2 (see subparagraph 2 f)).***];

77. As indicated in the footnote to subparagraph e), a definition of "collective investment vehicle" should be included if a provision dealing with collective investment vehicles is included in subparagraph f) of paragraph 2. That definition should identify the collective investment vehicles of each Contracting State to which that provision is applicable and could be drafted as follows:

> *the term "collective investment vehicle" means, in the case of [State A], a [ ] and, in the case of [State B], a [ ], as well as any other investment fund, arrangement or entity established in either Contracting State which the competent authorities of the Contracting States agree to regard as a collective investment vehicle for purposes of this paragraph;*

78. As explained in paragraph 6.22 of the Commentary on Article 1, it is intended that the open parts of that definition would include cross-references to relevant tax or securities law provisions of each State that would identify the CIVs to which subparagraph f) of paragraph 2 should apply.

The term "equivalent beneficiary"[1]

Simplified version

c) the term "equivalent beneficiary" means any person who would be entitled to an equivalent or more favourable benefit with respect to an item of income accorded by a Contracting State under the domestic law of that Contracting State, this Convention or any other international instrument as the benefit to be accorded to that item of income under this Convention, provided that, if that person is a resident of neither of the Contracting States, the first-mentioned Contracting State has a convention for the effective and comprehensive exchange of information relating to tax matters in effect with the state of which that person is a resident. For the purposes of determining whether a person is an equivalent beneficiary with respect to dividends, the person shall be deemed to hold the same capital, shares or voting powers, as the case may be, of the company paying the dividends as the company claiming the benefit with respect to the dividends holds those of the company paying the dividends.

Detailed version

[f) the term "equivalent beneficiary" means a resident of any other State, but only if that resident

i) A) would be entitled to all the benefits of a comprehensive convention for the avoidance of double taxation between that other State and the State from which the benefits of this Convention are claimed under provisions analogous to subparagraph a), b) or d), or subdivision i) of subparagraph c), of paragraph 2 of this Article, provided that if such convention does not contain a comprehensive limitation on benefits article, the person would be entitled to the benefits of this Convention by reason of subparagraph a), b), subdivision i) of subparagraph c), or subparagraph d) of paragraph 2 of this Article if such person were a resident of one of the Contracting States under Article 4 of this Convention; and

B) *with respect to income referred to in Articles 10, 11 and 12 of this Convention, would be entitled under such convention to a rate of tax with respect to the particular class of income for which benefits are being claimed under this Convention that is at least as low as the rate applicable under this Convention; or*

ii) *is a resident of a Contracting State that is entitled to the benefits of this Convention by reason of subparagraph a), b) or d), or subdivision i) of subparagraph c), of paragraph 2 of this Article.*]

[*Footnote 1: The inclusion of a definition of "equivalent beneficiary" will depend on whether paragraph 4 is included and whether that phrase is used in subparagraph f) of paragraph 2 dealing with collective investment vehicles.*]

Commentary on the detailed version

79. The definition of "equivalent beneficiary" is relevant for the purposes of the derivative benefits test in paragraph 4 but may also be relevant for the purposes of subparagraph f) of paragraph 2 depending on how that rule is drafted.

80. Under the definition, a person may qualify as an "equivalent beneficiary" in two alternative ways.

81. Under the first alternative, a person may be an equivalent beneficiary because it is entitled to equivalent benefits under a tax treaty between the State of source and a third State in which the person is a resident. This alternative has two requirements. Under the first requirement in subdivision i)A), the person must be entitled to equivalent benefits under an applicable tax treaty. To satisfy that requirement, the person must be entitled to all the benefits of a comprehensive tax treaty between the Contracting State from which benefits of the Convention are claimed and a third State under provisions that are analogous to the rules in subparagraphs a), b) or d), or subdivision i) of subparagraph c), of paragraph 2. If the treaty in question does not have a comprehensive limitation on benefits article, this requirement is met only if the person would be entitled to treaty benefits under the tests in subparagraphs a), b) or d), or subdivision i) of subparagraph c), of paragraph 2 if that person were a resident of one of the Contracting States.

82. The second requirement in subdivision i)B) applies only with respect to benefits applicable to dividends, interest and royalties. Under that additional requirement, the person must be entitled to a rate of tax that is at least as low as the tax rate that would apply under the Convention to such income. Thus, the rates to be compared are: (1) the rate of tax that the source State would have imposed if a resident of the other Contracting State who is a qualified person were the beneficial owner of the income; and (2) the rate of tax that the source State would have imposed if the third State resident received the income directly from the source State.

83. The requirement in subdivision i)A) that a person be entitled to "all the benefits" of a comprehensive tax treaty eliminates those persons that qualify for benefits with respect to only certain types of income. Assume, for example, that company CCO, a resident of State C, is the parent of ACO, a company resident of State A. CCO is engaged in the active conduct of a business in State C and,

for that reason, would be entitled to the benefits of a treaty between State C and State B if it received dividends directly from a State B subsidiary of ACO. This, however, is not sufficient for the purposes of the application of subdivision i)B) of the treaty between State A and State B. Also, CCO cannot be an equivalent beneficiary if it qualifies for benefits only with respect to certain income as a result of a "derivative benefits" provision in the treaty between State A and State C. However, it would be possible to look through CCO to its own parent company in order to determine whether that parent company is an equivalent beneficiary.

84. The second alternative for satisfying the "equivalent beneficiary" test in subdivision ii) is available only to residents of one of the Contracting States. These residents are equivalent beneficiaries if they are eligible for treaty benefits by reason of subparagraphs a), b) or d), or subdivision i) of subparagraph c), of paragraph 2. Thus, an individual resident of one Contracting State will be an equivalent beneficiary without regard to whether the individual would have been entitled to receive the same benefits if he had received the income directly. This second alternative clarifies that ownership by certain residents of a Contracting State would not disqualify a company from qualifying for treaty benefits under paragraph 4. Thus, for example, if 90 per cent of a company resident of State A is owned by five companies that are resident in State C and that satisfy the requirements of subdivision i) of the definition, and 10 per cent of the company is owned by an individual resident of State A or State B, then the company still can satisfy the requirements of subparagraph a) of paragraph 4.

The term "dual listed company arrangement"

Detailed version only

g) the term "dual listed company arrangement" means an arrangement pursuant to which two publicly listed companies, while maintaining their separate legal entity status, shareholdings and listings, align their strategic directions and the economic interests of their respective shareholders through:

i) the appointment of common (or almost identical) boards of directors, except where relevant regulatory requirements prevent this;

ii) management of the operations of the two companies on a unified basis;

iii) equalised distributions to shareholders in accordance with an equalisation ratio applying between the two companies, including in the event of a winding up of one or both of the companies;

iv) the shareholders of both companies voting in effect as a single decision-making body on substantial issues affecting their combined interests; and

v) cross-guarantees as to, or similar financial support for, each other's material obligations or operations except where the effect of the relevant regulatory requirements prevents such guarantees or financial support;

85. The term "dual listed company arrangement" is relevant for the purposes of the definition of the term "principal class of shares", which itself is relevant for the purposes of the provisions of subparagraph c) of paragraph 2 under which certain publicly-listed companies are "qualified persons".

86. The definition refers to an arrangement, adopted by certain publicly-listed companies, that reflect a commonality of management, operations, shareholders' rights, purpose and mission through a series of agreements between two parent companies, each with its own stock exchange listing, together with special provisions in their respective articles of association including in some cases, for example, the creation of special voting shares. Under these structures, the position of the parent company shareholders is, as far as possible, the same as if they held shares in a single company, with the same dividend entitlement and same rights to participate in the assets of the dual listed companies in the event of a winding up. The various parts of the definition refer to the various features that identify these arrangements.

The term "shares"

Detailed version only

h) with respect to entities that are not companies, the term "shares" means interests that are comparable to shares.

87. The Article does not contain an exhaustive definition of the term "shares", which, under paragraph 2 of Article 3, should generally have the meaning which it has under the domestic law of the State that applies the Article. Subparagraph h), however, provides that the term "shares", when used in the Article with respect to entities that do not issue shares (e.g. trusts), refers to interests that are comparable to shares. These will typically be beneficial interests that entitle their holders to a share of the income or assets of the entity.]

The term "related enterprise"

Simplified version only

d) A person shall be a related enterprise of another if, on the basis of all the facts and circumstances, one has control of the other or both are under the control of the same person or persons.

Mode of application to be determined by the competent authorities

Simplified version only

7. The competent authorities of the Contracting States may by mutual agreement settle the mode of application of this Article.

ii) Rules aimed at arrangements one of the principal purposes of which is to obtain treaty benefits

26. As previously indicated, the following rule, which incorporates principles already recognised in the Commentary on Article 1 of the OECD Model Tax Convention, provides a more general way to address treaty avoidance cases, including treaty-shopping situations, such as certain conduit financing arrangements, that are not covered by the specific

anti-abuse rule in subsection A.1(*a*)(*i*) above (the Commentary on the new rule includes a number of changes that were made to the Commentary included in the first version of this Report released in September 2014):

ARTICLE X

ENTITLEMENT TO BENEFITS

[*Paragraphs 1 to 6: see subsection* A.1(*a*)(*i*) *above*]

7. Notwithstanding the other provisions of this Convention, a benefit under this Convention shall not be granted in respect of an item of income or capital if it is reasonable to conclude, having regard to all relevant facts and circumstances, that obtaining that benefit was one of the principal purposes of any arrangement or transaction that resulted directly or indirectly in that benefit, unless it is established that granting that benefit in these circumstances would be in accordance with the object and purpose of the relevant provisions of this Convention.

Commentary

1. Paragraph 7 mirrors the guidance in paragraphs 9.5, 22, 22.1 and 22.2 of the Commentary on Article 1. According to that guidance, the benefits of a tax convention should not be available where one of the principal purposes of certain transactions or arrangements is to secure a benefit under a tax treaty and obtaining that benefit in these circumstances would be contrary to the object and purpose of the relevant provisions of the tax convention. Paragraph 7 incorporates the principles underlying these paragraphs into the Convention itself in order to allow States to address cases of improper use of the Convention even if their domestic law does not allow them to do so in accordance with paragraphs 22 and 22.1 of the Commentary on Article 1; it also confirms the application of these principles for States whose domestic law already allows them to address such cases.

2. The provisions of paragraph 7 have the effect of denying a benefit under a tax convention where one of the principal purposes of an arrangement or transaction that has been entered into is to obtain a benefit under the convention. Where this is the case, however, the last part of the paragraph allows the person to whom the benefit would otherwise be denied the possibility of establishing that obtaining the benefit in these circumstances would be in accordance with the object and purpose of the relevant provisions of this Convention.

3. Paragraph 7 supplements and does not restrict in any way the scope or application of the provisions of paragraphs 1 to 6 (the limitation-on-benefits rule): a benefit that is denied in accordance with these paragraphs is not a "benefit under the Convention" that paragraph 7 would also deny. Moreover, the guidance provided in the Commentary on paragraph 7 should not be used to interpret paragraphs 1 to 6 and vice-versa.

4. Conversely, the fact that a person is entitled to benefits under paragraphs 1 to 6 does not mean that these benefits cannot be denied under paragraph 7. Paragraphs 1 to 6 are rules that focus primarily on the legal nature, ownership

in, and general activities of, residents of a Contracting State. As illustrated by the example in the next paragraph, these rules do not imply that a transaction or arrangement entered into by such a resident cannot constitute an improper use of a treaty provision.

5. Paragraph 7 must be read in the context of paragraphs 1 to 6 and of the rest of the Convention, including its preamble. This is particularly important for the purposes of determining the object and purpose of the relevant provisions of the Convention. Assume, for instance, that a public company whose shares are regularly traded on a recognised stock exchange in the Contracting State of which the company is a resident derives income from the other Contracting State. As long as that company is a "qualified person" as defined in paragraph 2, it is clear that the benefits of the Convention should not be denied solely on the basis of the ownership structure of that company, e.g. because a majority of the shareholders in that company are not residents of the same State. The object and purpose of subparagraph 2 c) is to establish a threshold for the treaty entitlement of public companies whose shares are held by residents of different States. The fact that such a company is a qualified person does not mean, however, that benefits could not be denied under paragraph 7 for reasons that are unrelated to the ownership of the shares of that company. Assume, for instance, that such a public company is a bank that enters into a conduit financing arrangement intended to provide indirectly to a resident of a third State the benefit of lower source taxation under a tax treaty. In that case, paragraph 7 would apply to deny that benefit because subparagraph 2 c), when read in the context of the rest of the Convention and, in particular, its preamble, cannot be considered as having the purpose, shared by the two Contracting States, of authorising treaty-shopping transactions entered into by public companies.

6. The provisions of paragraph 7 establish that a Contracting State may deny the benefits of a tax convention where it is reasonable to conclude, having considered all the relevant facts and circumstances, that one of the principal purposes of an arrangement or transaction was for a benefit under a tax treaty to be obtained. The provision is intended to ensure that tax conventions apply in accordance with the purpose for which they were entered into, i.e. to provide benefits in respect of bona fide exchanges of goods and services, and movements of capital and persons as opposed to arrangements whose principal objective is to secure a more favourable tax treatment.

7. The term "benefit" includes all limitations (e.g. a tax reduction, exemption, deferral or refund) on taxation imposed on the State of source under Articles 6 through 22 of the Convention, the relief from double taxation provided by Article 23, and the protection afforded to residents and nationals of a Contracting State under Article 24 or any other similar limitations. This includes, for example, limitations on the taxing rights of a Contracting State in respect of dividends, interest or royalties arising in that State, and paid to a resident of the other State (who is the beneficial owner) under Article 10, 11 or 12. It also includes limitations on the taxing rights of a Contracting State over a capital gain derived from the alienation of movable property located in that State by a resident of the other State under Article 13. When a tax convention includes other limitations (such as a tax sparing provision), the provisions of this Article also apply to that benefit.

8. The phrase "that resulted directly or indirectly in that benefit" is deliberately broad and is intended to include situations where the person who claims the application of the benefits under a tax treaty may do so with respect to a transaction that is not the one that was undertaken for one of the principal purposes of obtaining that treaty benefit. This is illustrated by the following example:

> *TCo, a company resident of State T, has acquired all the shares and debts of SCo, a company resident of State S, that were previously held by SCo's parent company. These include a loan made to SCo at 4 per cent interest payable on demand. State T does not have a tax convention with State S and, therefore, any interest paid by SCo to TCo is subject to a withholding tax on interest at a rate of 25 per cent in accordance with the domestic law of State S. Under the State R-State S tax convention, however, there is no withholding tax on interest paid by a company resident of a Contracting State and beneficially owned by a company resident of the other State; also, that treaty does not include provisions similar to paragraphs 1 to 6. TCo decides to transfer the loan to RCo, a subsidiary resident of State R, in exchange for three promissory notes payable on demand on which interest is payable at 3.9 per cent.*

In this example, whilst RCo is claiming the benefits of the State R-State S treaty with respect to a loan that was entered into for valid commercial reasons, if the facts of the case show that one of the principal purposes of TCo in transferring its loan to RCo was for RCo to obtain the benefit of the State R-State S treaty, then the provision would apply to deny that benefit as that benefit would result indirectly from the transfer of the loan.

9. The terms "arrangement or transaction" should be interpreted broadly and include any agreement, understanding, scheme, transaction or series of transactions, whether or not they are legally enforceable. In particular they include the creation, assignment, acquisition or transfer of the income itself, or of the property or right in respect of which the income accrues. These terms also encompass arrangements concerning the establishment, acquisition or maintenance of a person who derives the income, including the qualification of that person as a resident of one of the Contracting States, and include steps that persons may take themselves in order to establish residence. An example of an "arrangement" would be where steps are taken to ensure that meetings of the board of directors of a company are held in a different country in order to claim that the company has changed its residence. One transaction alone may result in a benefit, or it may operate in conjunction with a more elaborate series of transactions that together result in the benefit. In both cases the provisions of paragraph 7 may apply.

10. To determine whether or not one of the principal purposes of any person concerned with an arrangement or transaction is to obtain benefits under the Convention, it is important to undertake an objective analysis of the aims and objects of all persons involved in putting that arrangement or transaction in place or being a party to it. What are the purposes of an arrangement or transaction is a question of fact which can only be answered by considering all circumstances surrounding the arrangement or event on a case by case basis. It is not necessary to find conclusive proof of the intent of a person concerned with an arrangement

or transaction, but it must be reasonable to conclude, after an objective analysis of the relevant facts and circumstances, that one of the principal purposes of the arrangement or transaction was to obtain the benefits of the tax convention. It should not be lightly assumed, however, that obtaining a benefit under a tax treaty was one of the principal purposes of an arrangement or transaction and merely reviewing the effects of an arrangement will not usually enable a conclusion to be drawn about its purposes. Where, however, an arrangement can only be reasonably explained by a benefit that arises under a treaty, it may be concluded that one of the principal purposes of that arrangement was to obtain the benefit.

11. A person cannot avoid the application of this paragraph by merely asserting that the arrangement or transaction was not undertaken or arranged to obtain the benefits of the Convention. All of the evidence must be weighed to determine whether it is reasonable to conclude that an arrangement or transaction was undertaken or arranged for such purpose. The determination requires reasonableness, suggesting that the possibility of different interpretations of the events must be objectively considered.

12. The reference to "one of the principal purposes" in paragraph 7 means that obtaining the benefit under a tax convention need not be the sole or dominant purpose of a particular arrangement or transaction. It is sufficient that at least one of the principal purposes was to obtain the benefit. For example, a person may sell a property for various reasons, but if before the sale, that person becomes a resident of one of the Contracting States and one of the principal purposes for doing so is to obtain a benefit under a tax convention, paragraph 7 could apply notwithstanding the fact that there may also be other principal purposes for changing the residence, such as facilitating the sale of the property or the re-investment of the proceeds of the alienation.

13. A purpose will not be a principal purpose when it is reasonable to conclude, having regard to all relevant facts and circumstances, that obtaining the benefit was not a principal consideration and would not have justified entering into any arrangement or transaction that has, alone or together with other transactions, resulted in the benefit. In particular, where an arrangement is inextricably linked to a core commercial activity, and its form has not been driven by considerations of obtaining a benefit, it is unlikely that its principal purpose will be considered to be to obtain that benefit. Where, however, an arrangement is entered into for the purpose of obtaining similar benefits under a number of treaties, it should not be considered that obtaining benefits under other treaties will prevent obtaining one benefit under one treaty from being considered a principal purpose for that arrangement. Assume, for example, that a taxpayer resident of State A enters into a conduit arrangement with a financial institution resident of State B in order for that financial institution to invest, for the ultimate benefit of that taxpayer, in bonds issued in a large number of States with which State B, but not State A, has tax treaties. If the facts and circumstances reveal that the arrangement has been entered into for the principal purpose of obtaining the benefits of these tax treaties, it should not be considered that obtaining a benefit under one specific treaty was not one of the principal purposes for that arrangement. Similarly, purposes related to the avoidance of domestic law should not be used to argue that obtaining a treaty benefit was merely accessory to such purposes.

14. The following examples illustrate the application of the paragraph (the examples included in paragraph 19 below should also be considered when determining whether and when the paragraph would apply in the case of conduit arrangements):

- *Example A: TCo, a company resident of State T, owns shares of SCo, a company listed on the stock exchange of State S. State T does not have a tax convention with State S and, therefore, any dividend paid by SCo to TCo is subject to a withholding tax on dividends of 25 per cent in accordance with the domestic law of State S. Under the State R-State S tax convention, however, there is no withholding tax on dividends paid by a company resident of a Contracting State and beneficially owned by a company resident of the other State. TCo enters into an agreement with RCo, an independent financial institution resident of State R, pursuant to which TCo assigns to RCo the right to the payment of dividends that have been declared but have not yet been paid by SCo.*

  In this example, in the absence of other facts and circumstances showing otherwise, it would be reasonable to conclude that one of the principal purposes for the arrangement under which TCo assigned the right to the payment of dividends to RCo was for RCo to obtain the benefit of the exemption from source taxation of dividends provided for by the State R-State S tax convention and it would be contrary to the object and purpose of the tax convention to grant the benefit of that exemption under this treaty-shopping arrangement.

- *Example B: SCo, a company resident of State S, is the subsidiary of TCo, a company resident of State T. State T does not have a tax convention with State S and, therefore, any dividend paid by SCo to TCo is subject to a withholding tax on dividends of 25 per cent in accordance with the domestic law of State S. Under the State R-State S tax convention, however, the applicable rate of withholding tax on dividends paid by a company of State S to a resident of State R is 5 per cent. TCo therefore enters into an agreement with RCo, a financial institution resident of State R and a qualified person under subparagraph 3 a) of this Article, pursuant to which RCo acquires the usufruct of newly issued non-voting preferred shares of SCo for a period of three years. TCo is the bare owner of these shares. The usufruct gives RCo the right to receive the dividends attached to these preferred shares. The amount paid by RCo to acquire the usufruct corresponds to the present value of the dividends to be paid on the preferred shares over the period of three years (discounted at the rate at which TCo could borrow from RCo).*

  In this example, in the absence of other facts and circumstances showing otherwise, it would be reasonable to conclude that one of the principal purposes for the arrangement under which RCo acquired the usufruct of the preferred shares issued by SCo was to obtain the benefit of the 5 per cent limitation applicable to the source taxation of dividends provided for by the State R-State S tax convention and it would be contrary to the object and purpose of the tax convention to grant the benefit of that limitation under this treaty-shopping arrangement.

- *Example C: RCo, a company resident of State R, is in the business of producing electronic devices and its business is expanding rapidly. It is now considering establishing a manufacturing plant in a developing country in order to benefit from lower manufacturing costs. After a preliminary review, possible locations in three different countries are identified. All three countries provide similar economic and political environments. After considering the fact that State S is the only one of these countries with which State R has a tax convention, the decision is made to build the plant in that State.*

  In this example, whilst the decision to invest in State S is taken in the light of the benefits provided by the State R-State S tax convention, it is clear that the principal purposes for making that investment and building the plant are related to the expansion of RCo's business and the lower manufacturing costs of that country. In this example, it cannot reasonably be considered that one of the principal purposes for building the plant is to obtain treaty benefits. In addition, given that a general objective of tax conventions is to encourage cross-border investment, obtaining the benefits of the State R-State S convention for the investment in the plant built in State S is in accordance with the object and purpose of the provisions of that convention.

- *Example D: RCo, a collective investment vehicle resident of State R, manages a diversified portfolio of investments in the international financial market. RCo currently holds 15 per cent of its portfolio in shares of companies resident of State S, in respect of which it receives annual dividends. Under the tax convention between State R and State S, the withholding tax rate on dividends is reduced from 30 per cent to 10 per cent.*

  RCo's investment decisions take into account the existence of tax benefits provided under State R's extensive tax convention network. A majority of investors in RCo are residents of State R, but a number of investors (the minority investors) are residents of States with which State S does not have a tax convention. Investors' decisions to invest in RCo are not driven by any particular investment made by RCo, and RCo's investment strategy is not driven by the tax position of its investors. RCo annually distributes almost all of its income to its investors and pays taxes in State R on income not distributed during the year.

  In making its decision to invest in shares of companies resident of State S, RCo considered the existence of a benefit under the State R-State S tax convention with respect to dividends, but this alone would not be sufficient to trigger the application of paragraph 7. The intent of tax treaties is to provide benefits to encourage cross-border investment and, therefore, to determine whether or not paragraph 7 applies to an investment, it is necessary to consider the context in which the investment was made. In this example, unless RCo's investment is part of an arrangement or relates to another transaction undertaken for a principal purpose of obtaining the benefit of the Convention, it would not be reasonable to deny the benefit of the State R-State S tax treaty to RCo.

- *Example E: RCo is a company resident of State R and, for the last 5 years, has held 24 per cent of the shares of company SCo, a resident of State S. Following the entry-into-force of a tax treaty between States R and S (Article 10 of which is identical to Article 10 of this Model), RCo decides to increase to 25 per cent its ownership of the shares of SCo. The facts and circumstances reveal that the decision to acquire these additional shares has been made primarily in order to obtain the benefit of the lower rate of tax provided by Article 10(2)a) of the treaty.*

  In that case, although one of the principal purposes for the transaction through which the additional shares are acquired is clearly to obtain the benefit of Article 10(2)a), paragraph 7 would not apply because it may be established that granting that benefit in these circumstances would be in accordance with the object and purpose of Article 10(2) a). That subparagraph uses an arbitrary threshold of 25 per cent for the purposes of determining which shareholders are entitled to the benefit of the lower rate of tax on dividends and it is consistent with this approach to grant the benefits of the subparagraph to a taxpayer who genuinely increases its participation in a company in order to satisfy this requirement.

- *Example F: TCO is a publicly-traded company resident of State T. TCO's information technology business, which was developed in State T, has grown considerably over the last few years as a result of an aggressive merger and acquisition policy pursued by TCO's management. RCO, a company resident of State R (a State that has concluded many tax treaties providing for no or low source taxation of dividends and royalties), is the family-owned holding company of a group that is also active in the information technology sector. Almost all the shares of RCO are owned by residents of State R who are relatives of the entrepreneur who launched and developed the business of the RCO group. RCO's main assets are shares of subsidiaries located in neighbouring countries, including SCO, a company resident of State S, as well as patents developed in State R and licensed to these subsidiaries. TCO, which has long been interested in acquiring the business of the RCO group and its portfolio of patents, has made an offer to acquire all the shares of RCO.*

  In this example, in the absence of other facts and circumstances showing otherwise, it would be reasonable to conclude that the principal purposes for the acquisition of RCO are related to the expansion of the business of the TCO group and do not include the obtaining of benefits under the treaty between States R and S. The fact that RCO acts primarily as a holding company does not change that result. It might well be that, after the acquisition of the shares of RCO, TCO's management will consider the benefits of the tax treaty concluded between State R and State S before deciding to keep in RCO the shares of SCO and the patents licensed to SCO. This, however, would not be a purpose related to the relevant transaction, which is the acquisition of the shares of RCO.

- *Example G: TCO, a company resident of State T, is a publicly-traded company resident of State T. It owns directly or indirectly a number of subsidiaries in different countries. Most of these companies carry on the business activities of the TCO group in local markets. In one region, TCO owns the shares of five such companies, each located in different neighbouring States. TCO is considering establishing a regional company for the purpose of providing group services to these companies, including management services such as accounting, legal advice and human resources; financing and treasury services such as managing currency risks and arranging hedging transactions, as well as some other non-financing related services. After a review of possible locations, TCO decides to establish the regional company, RCO, in State R. This decision is mainly driven by the skilled labour force, reliable legal system, business friendly environment, political stability, membership of a regional grouping, sophisticated banking industry and the comprehensive double taxation treaty network of State R, including its tax treaties with the five States in which TCO owns subsidiaries, which all provide low withholding tax rates.*

  In this example, merely reviewing the effects of the treaties on future payments by the subsidiaries to the regional company would not enable a conclusion to be drawn about the purposes for the establishment of RCO by TCO. Assuming that the intra-group services to be provided by RCO, including the making of decisions necessary for the conduct of its business, constitute a real business through which RCO exercises substantive economic functions, using real assets and assuming real risks, and that business is carried on by RCO through its own personnel located in State R, it would not be reasonable to deny the benefits of the treaties concluded between State R and the five States where the subsidiaries operate unless other facts would indicate that RCO has been established for other tax purposes or unless RCO enters into specific transactions to which paragraph 7 would otherwise apply (see also example F in paragraph 15 below with respect to the interest and other remuneration that RCO might derive from its group financing activities).

- *Example H: TCO is a company resident of State T that is listed on the stock exchange of State T. It is the parent company of a multinational enterprise that conducts a variety of business activities globally (wholesaling, retailing, manufacturing, investment, finance, etc.). Issues related to transportation, time differences, limited availability of personnel fluent in foreign languages and the foreign location of business partners make it difficult for TCO to manage its foreign activities from State T. TCO therefore establishes RCO, a subsidiary resident of State R (a country where there are developed international trade and financial markets as well as an abundance of highly-qualified human resources), as a base for developing its foreign business activities. RCO carries on diverse business activities such as wholesaling, retailing, manufacturing, financing and domestic and international investment. RCO possesses the human and financial resources (in various areas such as legal, financial, accounting, taxation, risk management, auditing and internal control) that are necessary to perform these activities. It is clear that RCO's activities constitute the active conduct of a business in State R.*

As part of its activities, RCO also undertakes the development of new manufacturing facilities in State S. For that purpose, it contributes equity capital and makes loans to SCO, a subsidiary resident of State S that RCO established for the purposes of owning these facilities. RCO will receive dividends and interest from SCO.

In this example, RCO has been established for business efficiency reasons and its financing of SCO through equity and loans is part of RCO's active conduct of a business in State R. Based on these facts and in the absence of other facts that would indicate that one of the principal purposes for the establishment of RCO or the financing of SCO was the obtaining of the benefits of the treaty between States R and S, paragraph 7 would not apply to these transactions.

- *Example I: RCO, a company resident of State R, is one of a number of collective management organisations that grant licenses on behalf of neighbouring right and copyright holders for playing music in public or for broadcasting that music on radio, television or the internet. SCO, a company resident of State S, carries on similar activities in State S. Performers and copyright holders from various countries appoint RCO or SCO as their agent to grant licenses and to receive royalties with respect to the copyrights and neighbouring rights that they hold; RCO and SCO distribute to each right holder the amount of royalties that they receive on behalf of that holder minus a commission (in most cases, the amount distributed to each holder is relatively small). RCO has an agreement with SCO through which SCO grants licenses to users in State S and distributes royalties to RCO with respect to the rights that RCO manages; RCO does the same in State R with respect to the rights that SCO manages. SCO has agreed with the tax administration of State S that it will process the royalty withholding tax on the payments that it makes to RCO based on the applicable treaties between State S and the State of residence of each right holder represented by RCO based on information provided by RCO since these right holders are the beneficial owners of the royalties paid by SCO to RCO.*

  In this example, it is clear that the arrangements between the right holders and RCO and SCO, and between SCO and RCO, have been put in place for the efficient management of the granting of licenses and collection of royalties with respect to a large number of small transactions. Whilst one of the purposes for entering into these arrangements may well be to ensure that withholding tax is collected at the correct treaty rate without the need for each individual right holder to apply for a refund on small payments, which would be cumbersome and expensive, it is clear that such purpose, which serves to promote the correct and efficient application of tax treaties, would

be in accordance with the object and purpose of the relevant provisions of the applicable treaties.

- ***Example J: RCO is a company resident of State R. It has successfully submitted a bid for the construction of a power plant for SCO, an independent company resident of State S. That construction project is expected to last 22 months. During the negotiation of the contract, the project is divided into two different contracts, each lasting 11 months. The first contract is concluded with RCO and the second contract is concluded with SUBCO, a recently incorporated wholly-owned subsidiary of RCO resident of State R. At the request of SCO, which wanted to ensure that RCO would be contractually liable for the performance of the two contracts, the contractual arrangements are such that RCO is jointly and severally liable with SUBCO for the performance of SUBCO's contractual obligations under the SUBCO-SCO contract.***

  In this example, in the absence of other facts and circumstances showing otherwise, it would be reasonable to conclude that one of the principal purposes for the conclusion of the separate contract under which SUBCO agreed to perform part of the construction project was for RCO and SUBCO to each obtain the benefit of the rule in paragraph 3 of Article 5 of the State R-State S tax convention. Granting the benefit of that rule in these circumstances would be contrary to the object and purpose of that paragraph as the time limitation of that paragraph would otherwise be meaningless.

15. In a number of States, the application of the general anti-abuse rule found in domestic law is subject to some form of approval process. In some cases, the process provides for an internal acceleration of disputes on such provisions to senior officials in the administration. In other cases, the process allows for advisory panels to provide their views to the administration on the application of the rule. These types of approval processes reflect the serious nature of disputes in this area and promote overall consistency in the application of the rule. States may wish to establish a similar form of administrative process that would ensure that paragraph 7 is only applied after approval at a senior level within the administration.

16. Also, some States consider that where a person is denied a treaty benefit in accordance with paragraph 7, the competent authority of the Contracting State that would otherwise have granted this benefit should have the possibility of treating that person as being entitled to this benefit, or to different benefits with respect to the relevant item of income or capital, if such benefits would have been granted to that person in the absence of the transaction or arrangement that triggered the application of paragraph 7. In order to allow that possibility, such States are free to include the following additional paragraph in their bilateral treaties:

> ***8. Where a benefit under this Convention is denied to a person under paragraph 7, the competent authority of the Contracting State that would otherwise have granted this benefit shall nevertheless treat that person as being entitled to this benefit, or to different benefits with respect to a specific item of income or capital, if such competent authority, upon***

request from that person and after consideration of the relevant facts and circumstances, determines that such benefits would have been granted to that person in the absence of the transaction or arrangement referred to in paragraph 7. The competent authority of the Contracting State to which the request has been made will consult with the competent authority of the other State before rejecting a request made under this paragraph by a resident of that other State.

17. For the purpose of this alternative provision, the determination that benefits would have been granted in the absence of the transaction or arrangement referred to in paragraph 7 and the determination of the benefits that should be granted are left to the discretion of the competent authority to which the request is made. The alternative provision grants broad discretion to the competent authority for the purposes of these determinations. The provision does require, however, that the competent authority must consider the relevant facts and circumstances before reaching a decision and must consult the competent authority of the other Contracting State before rejecting a request to grant benefits if that request was made by a resident of that other State. The first requirement seeks to ensure that the competent authority will consider each request on its own merits whilst the requirement that the competent authority of the other Contracting State be consulted if the request is made by a resident of that other State should ensure that Contracting States treat similar cases in a consistent manner and can justify their decision on the basis of the facts and circumstances of the particular case. This consultation process does not, however, require that the competent authority to which the request was presented obtain the agreement of the competent authority that is consulted.

18. The following example illustrates the application of this alternative provision. Assume that an individual who is a resident of State R and who owns shares in a company resident of State S assigns the right to receive dividends declared by that company to another company resident of State R which owns more than 10 per cent of the capital of the paying company for the principal purpose of obtaining the reduced rate of source taxation provided for in subparagraph a) of paragraph 2 of Article 10. In such a case, if it is determined that the benefit of that subparagraph should be denied pursuant to paragraph 7, the alternative provision would allow the competent authority of State S to grant the benefit of the reduced rate provided for in subparagraph b) of paragraph 2 of Article 10 if that competent authority determined that such benefit would have been granted in the absence of the assignment to another company of the right to receive dividends.

19. For various reasons, some States may be unable to accept the rule included in paragraph 7. In order to effectively address all forms of treaty-shopping, however, these States will need to supplement the limitation-on-benefits rule of paragraphs 1 to 6 by rules that will address treaty-shopping strategies commonly referred to as "conduit arrangements" that would not be caught by these paragraphs. These rules would deal with such conduit arrangements by denying the benefits of the provisions of the Convention, or of some of them (e.g. those of Articles 7, 10, 11, 12 and 21), in respect of any income obtained under, or as part of, a conduit arrangement. They could also take the form of domestic anti-abuse rules or judicial doctrines that would achieve a similar result. The following are examples of conduit arrangements that would need to be addressed by such rules as well as examples of transactions that should not be considered to be conduit arrangements for that purpose:

- *Example A: RCO a publicly-traded company resident of State R, owns all of the shares of SCO, a company resident of State S. TCo, a company resident of State T, which does not have a tax treaty with State S, would like to purchase a minority interest in SCO but believes that the domestic withholding tax on dividends levied by State S would make the investment uneconomic. RCO proposes that SCO instead issue to RCO preferred shares paying a fixed return of 4 per cent plus a contingent return of 20 per cent of SCO's net profits. The maturity of the preferred shares is 20 years. TCo will enter into a separate contract with RCO pursuant to which it will pay to RCO an amount equal to the issue price of the preferred shares and will receive from RCO after 20 years the redemption price of the shares. During the 20 years, RCO will pay to TCO an amount equal to 3.75 per cent of the issue price plus 20 per cent of SCO's net profits.*

  This arrangement constitutes a conduit arrangement that should be addressed by the rules referred to above because one of the principal purposes for RCO participating in the transaction was to achieve a reduction of the withholding tax for TCO.

- *Example B: SCO, a company resident of State S, has issued only one class of shares that is 100 per cent owned by RCO, a company resident of State R. RCO also has only one class of shares outstanding, all of which is owned by TCO, a company resident of State T, which does not have a tax treaty with State S. RCO is engaged in the manufacture of electronics products, and SCO serves as RCO's exclusive distributor in State S. Under paragraph 3 of the limitation-of-benefits rule, RCO will be entitled to benefits with respect to dividends received from SCO, even though the shares of RCO are owned by a resident of a third country.*

  This example refers to a normal commercial structure where RCO and SCO carry on real economic activities in States R and S. The payment of dividends by subsidiaries such as SCO is a normal business transaction. In the absence of evidence showing that one of the principal purposes for setting up that structure was to flow-through dividends from SCO to TCO, this structure would not constitute a conduit arrangement.

- *Example C: TCO, a company resident of State T, which does not have a tax treaty with State S, loans 1 000 000 to SCO, a company resident of State S that is a wholly-owned subsidiary of TCO, in exchange for a note issued by SCO. TCO later realises that it can avoid the withholding tax on interest levied by State S by assigning the note to its wholly-owned subsidiary RCO, a resident of State R (the treaty between States R and S does not allow source taxation of interest in certain circumstances). TCO therefore assigns the note to RCO in exchange for a note issued by RCO to TCO. The note issued by SCO pays interest at 7 per cent and the note issued by RCO pays interest at 6 per cent.*

The transaction through which RCO acquired the note issued by SCO constitutes a conduit arrangement because it was structured to eliminate the withholding tax that TCO would otherwise have paid to State S.

- *Example D: TCO, a company resident of State T, which does not have a tax treaty with State S, owns all of the shares of SCO, a company resident of State S. TCO has for a long time done all of its banking with RCO, a bank resident of State R which is unrelated to TCO and SCO, because the banking system in State T is relatively unsophisticated. As a result, TCO tends to maintain a large deposit with RCO. When SCO needs a loan to fund an acquisition, TCO suggests that SCO deal with RCO, which is already familiar with the business conducted by TCO and SCO. SCO discusses the loan with several different banks, all on terms similar to those offered by RCO, but eventually enters into the loan with RCO, in part because interest paid to RCO would not be subject to withholding tax in State S pursuant to the treaty between States S and R, whilst interest paid to banks resident of State T would be subject to tax in State S.*

  The fact that benefits of the treaty between State R and S are available if SCO borrows from RCO, and that similar benefits might not be available if it borrowed elsewhere, is clearly a factor in SCO's decision (which may be influenced by advice given to it by TCO, its 100 per cent shareholder). It may even be a decisive factor, in the sense that, all else being equal, the availability of treaty benefits may swing the balance in favour of borrowing from RCO rather than from another lender. However, whether the obtaining of treaty benefits was one of the principal purposes of the transaction would have to be determined by reference to the particular facts and circumstances. In the facts presented above, RCO is unrelated to TCO and SCO and there is no indication that the interest paid by SCO flows through to TCO one way or another. The fact that TCO has historically maintained large deposits with RCO is also a factor that indicates that the loan to SCO is not matched by a specific deposit from TCO. On the specific facts as presented, the transaction would therefore likely not constitute a conduit arrangement.

  If, however, RCO's decision to lend to SCO was dependent on TCO providing a matching collateral deposit to secure the loan so that RCO would not have entered into the transaction on substantially the same terms in the absence of that deposit, the facts would indicate that TCO was indirectly lending to SCO by routing the loan through a bank of State R and, in that case, the transaction would constitute a conduit arrangement.

- *Example E: RCO, a publicly-traded company resident of State R, is the holding company for a manufacturing group in a highly competitive technological field. The manufacturing group conducts research in subsidiaries located around the world. Any patents developed in a subsidiary are licensed by the subsidiary to RCO, which then licenses the technology to its subsidiaries that need it. RCO keeps only a small spread with respect to the royalties it receives, so that most of the profit goes to the subsidiary that incurred the risk with respect to developing the technology. TCO, a company located in a State with which State S does not have a tax treaty, has developed a process that will substantially increase the profitability of all of RCO's subsidiaries, including SCO, a company resident of State S. According to its usual practice, RCO licenses the technology and sub-licenses the technology to its subsidiaries. SCO pays a royalty to RCO, substantially all of which is paid to TCO.*

In this example, there is no indication that RCO established its licensing business in order to reduce the withholding tax payable in State S. Because RCO is conforming to the standard commercial organisation and behaviour of the group in the way that it structures its licensing and sub-licensing activities and assuming the same structure is employed with respect to other subsidiaries carrying out similar activities in countries which have treaties which offer similar or more favourable benefits, the arrangement between SCO, RCO and TCO does not constitute a conduit arrangement.

- *Example F: TCO is a publicly-traded company resident of State T, which does not have a tax treaty with State S. TCO is the parent of a worldwide group of companies, including RCO, a company resident of State R, and SCO, a company resident of State S. SCO is engaged in the active conduct of a trade or business in State S. RCO is responsible for co-ordinating the financing of all of the subsidiaries of TCO. RCO maintains a centralised cash management accounting system for TCO and its subsidiaries in which it records all intercompany payables and receivables. RCO is responsible for disbursing or receiving any cash payments required by transactions between its affiliates and unrelated parties. RCO enters into interest rate and foreign exchange contracts as necessary to manage the risks arising from mismatches in incoming and outgoing cash flows. The activities of RCO are intended (and reasonably can be expected) to reduce transaction costs and overhead and other fixed costs. RCO has 50 employees, including clerical and other back office personnel, located in State R; this number of employees reflects the size of the business activities of RCO. TCO lends to RCO 15 million in currency A (worth 10 million in currency B) in exchange for a 10-year note that pays 5 per cent interest annually. On the same day, RCO lends 10 million in currency B to SCO in exchange for a 10-year note that pays 5 per cent interest annually. RCO does not enter into a long-term hedging transaction with respect to these financing transactions, but manages the interest rate and currency risk arising from the transactions on a daily, weekly or quarterly basis by entering into forward currency contracts.*

  In this example, RCO appears to be carrying on a real business performing substantive economic functions, using real assets and assuming real risks; it is also performing significant activities with respect to the transactions with TCO and SCO, which appear to be typical of RCO's normal treasury business. RCO also appears to be bearing the interest rate and currency risk. Based on these facts and in

the absence of other facts that would indicate that one of the principal purposes for these loans was the avoidance of withholding tax in State S, the loan from TCO to RCO and the loan from RCO to SCO do not constitute a conduit arrangement.

b) Other situations where a person seeks to circumvent treaty limitations

27. Apart from the requirement that a person be a resident of a Contracting State, other conditions must be satisfied in order to obtain the benefit of certain provisions of tax treaties. In certain cases, it may be possible to enter into transactions for the purposes of satisfying these conditions in circumstances where it would be inappropriate to grant the relevant treaty benefits. Although the general anti-abuse rule in subsection A.1(*a*)(*ii*) above will be useful in addressing such situations, targeted specific treaty anti-abuse rules generally provide greater certainty for both taxpayers and tax administrations. Such rules are already found in some Articles of the Model Tax Convention (see, for example, Articles 13(4) and 17(2)). In addition, the Commentary suggests the inclusion of other anti-abuse provisions in certain circumstances (see, for example, paragraphs 16 and 17 of the Commentary on Article 10). Other anti-abuse provisions are found in bilateral treaties concluded by OECD and non-OECD countries.

28. The following are examples of situations with respect to which specific treaty anti-abuse rules may be helpful and proposals for changes intended to address some of these situations.

i) Splitting-up of contracts

29. Paragraph 18 of the Commentary on Article 5 indicates that "[t]he twelve-month threshold [*of Article 5(3)*] has given rise to abuses; it has sometimes been found that enterprises (mainly contractors or subcontractors working on the continental shelf or engaged in activities connected with the exploration and exploitation of the continental shelf) divided their contracts up into several parts, each covering a period less than twelve months and attributed to a different company which was, however, owned by the same group."

30. The addition to the OECD Model of the PPT rule included in this Report will help address this issue, as shown by example J of the Commentary on that rule. In addition, the Report on Action 7 (*Preventing the Artificial Avoidance of Permanent Establishment Status*, OECD, 2015b)[12] puts forward changes to the Commentary on Article 5 that will also deal with the issue.

ii) Hiring-out of labour cases

31. Hiring-out of labour cases, where the taxpayer attempts to obtain inappropriately the benefits of the exemption from source taxation provided for in Article 15(2), are dealt with in paragraphs 8.1 to 8.28 of the Commentary on Article 15. It was concluded that the guidance already found in these paragraphs, and in particular the alternative provision found in paragraph 8.3 of that Commentary, dealt adequately with this type of treaty abuse.

iii) Transactions intended to avoid dividend characterisation

32. In some cases, transactions may be entered into for the purpose of avoiding domestic law rules that characterise a certain item of income as a dividend and to benefit from a treaty characterisation of that income (e.g. as capital gain) that prevents source taxation.

33. As part of its work on hybrid mismatch arrangements, Working Party 1 has examined whether the treaty definitions of dividends and interest could be amended, as is done in some treaties, in order to permit the application of domestic law rules that characterise an item of income as such. Although it was concluded that such a change would have a very limited impact with respect to hybrid mismatch arrangements, it was decided to further examine the possibility of making such changes after the completion of the work on the BEPS Action Plan.

iv) Dividend transfer transactions

34. In these transactions, a taxpayer entitled to the 15 per cent portfolio rate of Article 10(2)b) seeks to obtain the 5 per cent direct dividend rate of Article 10(2)a) or the 0 per cent rate that some bilateral conventions provide for dividends paid to pension funds (see paragraph 69 of the Commentary on Article 18).

35. Paragraphs 16 and 17 of the Commentary on Article 10 deal with transactions through which a taxpayer tries to access the lower rate of 5 per cent applicable to dividends:

> 16. Subparagraph *a)* of paragraph 2 does not require that the company receiving the dividends must have owned at least 25 per cent of the capital for a relatively long time before the date of the distribution. This means that all that counts regarding the holding is the situation prevailing at the time material for the coming into existence of the liability to the tax to which paragraph 2 applies, i.e. in most cases the situation existing at the time when the dividends become legally available to the shareholders. The primary reason for this resides in the desire to have a provision which is applicable as broadly as possible. To require the parent company to have possessed the minimum holding for a certain time before the distribution of the profits could involve extensive inquiries. Internal laws of certain OECD member countries provide for a minimum period during which the recipient company must have held the shares to qualify for exemption or relief in respect of dividends received. In view of this, Contracting States may include a similar condition in their conventions.
>
> 17. The reduction envisaged in subparagraph a) of paragraph 2 should not be granted in cases of abuse of this provision, for example, where a company with a holding of less than 25 per cent has, shortly before the dividends become payable, increased its holding primarily for the purpose of securing the benefits of the abovementioned provision, or otherwise, where the qualifying holding was arranged primarily in order to obtain the reduction. To counteract such manoeuvres Contracting States may find it appropriate to add to subparagraph a) a provision along the following lines:
>
>> provided that this holding was not acquired primarily for the purpose of taking advantage of this provision.

36. It was concluded that in order to deal with such transactions, a minimum shareholding period should be included in subparagraph *a)* of Article 10(2), which should therefore be amended to read as follows:

> ***a) 5 per cent of the gross amount of the dividends if the beneficial owner is a company (other than a partnership) which holds directly at least 25 per cent of the capital of the company paying the dividends throughout a 365 day period that includes the day of the payment of the dividend (for the purpose of computing that period, no account shall be taken of changes of ownership that would directly result from a***

corporate reorganisation, such as a merger or divisive reorganisation, of the company that holds the shares or that pays the dividend);

37. It was also concluded that additional anti-abuse rules should be included in Article 10 to deal with cases where certain intermediary entities established in the State of source are used to take advantage of the treaty provisions that lower the source taxation of dividends.

38. For example, paragraph 67.4 of the Commentary on Article 10 includes an alternative provision that may be included to prevent access to

- the 5 per cent rate in the case of dividends paid by a domestic REIT to a non-resident portfolio investor, and
- both the 5 per cent and the 15 per cent rates in the case of dividends paid by a domestic REIT to a non-resident investor who holds directly or indirectly more than 10 per cent of the REIT's capital.

39. Another example, found in U.S. treaty practice, is a provision that denies the application of the 5 per cent rate in the case of dividends paid to a non-resident company by a U.S. Regulated Investment Company (RIC) even if that non-resident company holds more than 10 per cent of the shares of the RIC.

40. Based on these examples, where the domestic law of a Contracting State allows the possibility that portfolio investments in shares of companies of that State be made through certain collective investment vehicles which are established in that State and which do not pay tax on their investment income so that a non-resident investor in such a vehicle is able to access the lower treaty rate applicable to dividends with respect to distributions made by that collective investment vehicle, it is recommended that a specific anti-abuse rule be included in Article 10. Such a rule might be drafted along the following lines:

> Subparagraph 2 *a)* shall not apply to dividends paid by a resident of [*name of the State*] that is a [*description of the type of collective investment vehicle to which that rule should apply*]

v) Transactions that circumvent the application of Article 13(4)

41. Article 13(4) allows the Contracting State in which immovable property is situated to tax capital gains realised by a resident of the other State on shares of companies that derive more than 50 per cent of their value from such immovable property.

42. Paragraph 28.5 of the Commentary on Article 13 already provides that States may want to consider extending the provision to cover not only gains from shares but also gains from the alienation of interests in other entities, such as partnerships or trusts, which would address one form of abuse. It was agreed that Article 13(4) should be amended to include such wording.

43. There might also be cases, however, where assets are contributed to an entity shortly before the sale of the shares or other interests in that entity in order to dilute the proportion of the value of these shares or interests that is derived from immovable property situated in one Contracting State. In order to address such cases, it was agreed that Article 13(4) should be amended to refer to situations where shares or similar interest derive their value primarily from immovable property at any time during a certain period as opposed to at the time of the alienation only.

44. The following revised version of paragraph 4 of Article 13 incorporates these changes:

> 4. Gains derived by a resident of a Contracting State from the alienation of shares ***or comparable interests, such as interests in a partnership or trust, may be taxed in the other Contracting State if, at any time during the 365 days preceding the alienation, these shares or comparable interests derived*** ~~deriving~~ more than 50 per cent of their value directly or indirectly from immovable property, ***as defined in Article 6,*** situated in ***that*** ~~the~~ other State ~~may be taxed in that other State~~.

vi) Tie-breaker rule for determining the treaty residence of dual-resident persons other than individuals

45. One of the key limitations on the granting of treaty benefits is the requirement that a person be a resident of a Contracting State for the purposes of the relevant tax treaty. Under Article 4(1) of the OECD Model Tax Convention, the treaty residence of a person is dependent on the domestic tax laws of each Contracting State, which may result in a person being resident of both States. In such cases, Article 4(2) determines a single treaty residence in the case of individuals. Article 4(3), which does the same for persons other than individuals, provides that the dual-resident person "shall be deemed to be a resident only of the State in which its place of effective management is situated".

46. When this rule was originally included in the 1963 *Draft Convention*, the OECD Fiscal Committee expressed the view that "it may be rare in practice for a company, etc. to be subject to tax as a resident in more than one State"[13] but because that was possible, "special rules as to the preference" were needed.

47. The 2008 Update to the OECD Model Tax Convention introduced an alternative version of Article 4(3) (see paragraphs 24 and 24.1 of the Commentary on Article 4) according to which the competent authorities of the Contracting States shall, having regard to a number of relevant factors, endeavour to determine by mutual agreement the State of which the person is a resident for the purposes of the Convention. When that alternative was discussed, the view of many countries was that cases where a company is a dual-resident often involve tax avoidance arrangements. For that reason, the current rule found in Article 4(3) should be replaced by the alternative found in the Commentary, which allows a case-by-case solution of these cases.

48. The following are the changes that will be made to the OECD Model Tax Convention in order to implement that decision (these changes take account of modifications that were made to the Commentary included in the first version of this Report released in September 2014):

Replace paragraph 3 of Article 4 of the Model Tax Convention by the following:

> 3. Where by reason of the provisions of paragraph 1 a person other than an individual is a resident of both Contracting States, ~~then it shall be deemed to be a resident only of the State in which its place of effective management is situated.~~ ***the competent authorities of the Contracting States shall endeavour to determine by mutual agreement the Contracting State of which such person shall be deemed to be a resident for the purposes of the Convention, having regard to its place of effective management, the place where it is incorporated or otherwise constituted and any other relevant factors. In the absence of such agreement, such person shall not be entitled to any relief or exemption from tax provided by this Convention except to the extent and in such manner as may be agreed upon by the competent authorities of the Contracting States.***

Replace paragraphs 21 to 24.1 of the Commentary on Article 4 by the following:

21. This paragraph concerns companies and other bodies of persons, irrespective of whether they are or not legal persons. Cases where a company, etc. is subject to tax as a resident in more than one State may occur if, for instance, one State attaches importance to the registration and the other State to the place of effective management. So, in the case of companies, etc., also, special rules as to the preference must be established.

22. ***When paragraph 3 was first drafted, it was considered that i***~~I~~t would not be an adequate solution to attach importance to a purely formal criterion like registration~~.~~ ***and preference was given to a rule based on the place of effective management, which was intended to be based on*** ~~Therefore paragraph 3 attaches importance to~~ the place where the company, etc. ***was***~~is~~ actually managed.

23. ~~The formulation of the preference criterion in the case of persons other than individuals was considered in particular in connection with the taxation of income from shipping, inland waterways transport and air transport. A number of conventions for the avoidance of double taxation on such income accord the taxing power to the State in which the "place of management" of the enterprise is situated; other conventions attach importance to its "place of effective management", others again to the "fiscal domicile of the operator".~~ ***In [2014], however, the Committee on Fiscal Affairs recognised that although situations of double residence of entities other than individuals were relatively rare, there had been a number of tax avoidance cases involving dual resident companies. It therefore concluded that a better solution to the issue of dual residence of entities other than individuals was to deal with such situations on a case-by-case basis.***

24. As a result of these considerations, ***the current version of paragraph 3 provides that the competent authorities of the Contracting States shall endeavour to resolve by mutual agreement cases of dual residence of a person other than an individual.*** ~~the "place of effective management" has been adopted as the preference criterion for persons other than individuals. The place of effective management is the place where key management and commercial decisions that are necessary for the conduct of the entity's business as a whole are in substance made. All relevant facts and circumstances must be examined to determine the place of effective management. An entity may have more than one place of management, but it can have only one place of effective management at any one time.~~

24.1 ~~Some countries, however, consider that cases of dual residence of persons who are not individuals are relatively rare and should be dealt with on a case-by-case basis. Some countries also consider that such a case-by-case approach is the best way to deal with the difficulties in determining the place of effective management of a legal person that may arise from the use of new communication technologies. These countries are free to leave the question of the residence of these persons to be settled by the competent authorities, which can be done by replacing the paragraph by the following provision:~~

> ~~3. Where by reason of the provisions of paragraph 1 a person other than an individual is a resident of both Contracting States, the competent authorities of the Contracting States shall endeavour to determine by mutual agreement the Contracting State of which such person shall be deemed to be a resident for the purposes of the Convention, having regard to its place of effective management, the place where it is incorporated or otherwise constituted and~~

> ~~any other relevant factors. In the absence of such agreement, such person shall not be entitled to any relief or exemption from tax provided by this Convention except to the extent and in such manner as may be agreed upon by the competent authorities of the Contracting State.~~

Competent authorities having to apply ***paragraph 3*** ~~such a provision to determine the residence of a legal person for purposes of the Convention~~ would be expected to take account of various factors, such as where the meetings of ***the person's*** ~~its~~ board of directors or equivalent body are usually held, where the chief executive officer and other senior executives usually carry on their activities, where the senior day-to-day management of the person is carried on, where the person's headquarters are located, which country's laws govern the legal status of the person, where its accounting records are kept, whether determining that the legal person is a resident of one of the Contracting States but not of the other for the purpose of the Convention would carry the risk of an improper use of the provisions of the Convention etc. Countries that consider that the competent authorities should not be given the discretion to solve such cases of dual residence without an indication of the factors to be used for that purpose may want to supplement the provision to refer to these or other factors that they consider relevant. [*the next sentence has been moved to new paragraph 24.2; the last sentence of the paragraph has been moved to new paragraph 24.3*]

24.2 ~~Also, since the~~ ***A determination under paragraph 3*** ~~application of the provision would~~ ***will*** normally be requested by the person concerned through the mechanism provided for under paragraph 1 of Article 25~~, the~~. ***Such a*** request ***may be made as soon as it is probable that the person will be considered a resident of each Contracting State under paragraph 1. Due to the notification requirement in paragraph 1 of Article 25, it*** should ***in any event*** be made within three years from the first notification to that person ***of taxation measures taken by one or both States that indicate that reliefs or exemptions have been denied to that person because of its dual-residence status without the competent authorities having previously endeavoured to determine a single State of residence under paragraph 3. The competent authorities to which a request for determination of residence is made under paragraph 3 should deal with it expeditiously and should communicate their response to the taxpayer as soon as possible.***

24.3 Since the facts on which a decision will be based may change over time, the competent authorities that reach a decision under that provision should clarify which period of time is covered by that decision.

24.4 The last sentence of paragraph 3 provides that in the absence of a determination by the competent authorities, the dual-resident person shall not be entitled to any relief or exemption under the Convention except to the extent and in such manner as may be agreed upon by the competent authorities. This will not, however, prevent the taxpayer from being considered a resident of each Contracting State for purposes other than granting treaty reliefs or exemptions to that person. This will mean, for example, that the condition in subparagraph b) of paragraph 2 of Article 15 will not be met with respect to an employee of that person who is a resident of either Contracting State exercising employment activities in the other State. Similarly, if the person is a company, it will be considered to be a resident of each State for the purposes of the application of Article 10 to dividends that it will pay.

24.5~~2~~ Some States, however, consider that it is preferable to deal with cases of dual residence of entities through the rule based on the "place of effective management" that was included in the Convention before [next update]. These States also consider that this rule can be interpreted in a way that prevents it from being abused. States that share that view and that agree on how the concept of "place of effective management" should be interpreted are free to include in their bilateral treaty the following version of paragraph 3:

> ***Where by reason of the provisions of paragraph 1 a person other than an individual is a resident of both Contracting States, then it shall be deemed to be a resident only of the State in which its place of effective management is situated.***

vii) Anti-abuse rule for permanent establishments situated in third States

49. Paragraph 32 of the Commentary on Article 10, paragraph 25 of the Commentary on Article 11 and paragraph 21 of the Commentary on Article 12 refer to potential abuses that may result from the transfer of shares, debt-claims, rights or property to permanent establishments set up solely for that purpose in countries that offer preferential treatment to the income from such assets. Where the State of residence exempts, or taxes at low rates, profits of such permanent establishments situated in third States, the State of source should not be expected to grant treaty benefits with respect to that income.

50. The last part of paragraph 71 of the Commentary on Article 24 deals with that situation and suggests that an anti-abuse provision could be included in bilateral conventions to protect the State of source from having to grant treaty benefits where income obtained by a permanent establishment situated in a third State is not taxed normally in that State:

> 71. … Another question that arises with triangular cases is that of abuses. If the Contracting State of which the enterprise is a resident exempts from tax the profits of the permanent establishment located in the other Contracting State, there is a danger that the enterprise will transfer assets such as shares, bonds or patents to permanent establishments in States that offer very favourable tax treatment, and in certain circumstances the resulting income may not be taxed in any of the three States. To prevent such practices, which may be regarded as abusive, a provision can be included in the convention between the State of which the enterprise is a resident and the third State (the State of source) stating that an enterprise can claim the benefits of the convention only if the income obtained by the permanent establishment situated in the other State is taxed normally in the State of the permanent establishment.

51. It was concluded that a specific anti-abuse provision should be included in the Model Tax Convention to deal with that and similar triangular cases where income attributable to the permanent establishment in a third State is subject to low taxation.

52. The provision and related Commentary included below, which were intended to be used for that purpose, were included in the first version of this Report that was released in September 2014. Subsequent work, however, revealed that changes were required with respect to different aspects of that provision. At the end of May 2015, the United States released a new version of a similar provision[14] for public comments to be sent by 15 September 2015. When that new version was discussed, it was agreed that it should be further examined once finalised by the United States in the light of the comments that will

be received on it. For that reason, the provision below and its Commentary will need to be reviewed and the final version of the provision and its Commentary will therefore be produced in the first part of 2016, which will allow the new provision to be considered as part of the negotiation of the multilateral instrument that will implement the results of the work on treaty issues mandated by the BEPS Action Plan. The following should therefore be considered as a draft subject to changes:

> [*Where*
>
> ***a)*** ***an enterprise of a Contracting State derives income from the other Contracting State and such income is attributable to a permanent establishment of the enterprise situated in a third jurisdiction, and***
>
> ***b)*** ***the profits attributable to that permanent establishment are exempt from tax in the first-mentioned State***
>
> ***the tax benefits that would otherwise apply under the other provisions of the Convention will not apply to any item of income on which the tax in the third jurisdiction is less than 60 per cent of the tax that would be imposed in the first-mentioned State if the income were earned or received in that State by the enterprise and were not attributable to the permanent establishment in the third jurisdiction. In such a case***
>
> ***c)*** ***any dividends, interest, or royalties to which the provisions of this paragraph apply shall remain taxable according to the domestic law of the other State but the tax charged in that State shall not exceed [rate to be determined] per cent of the gross amount thereof, and***
>
> ***d)*** ***any other income to which the provisions of this paragraph apply shall remain taxable according to the domestic law of the other State, notwithstanding any other provision of the Convention.***
>
> ***The preceding provisions of this paragraph shall not apply if the income derived from the other State is***
>
> ***e)*** ***derived in connection with or is incidental to the active conduct of a business carried on through the permanent establishment (other than the business of making, managing or simply holding investments for the enterprise's own account, unless these activities are banking, insurance or securities activities carried on by a bank, insurance enterprise or registered securities dealer, respectively), or***
>
> ***f)*** ***royalties that are received as compensation for the use of, or the right to use, intangible property produced or developed by the enterprise through the permanent establishment.***

Commentary on the provision

> ***1. As mentioned in paragraph 32 of the Commentary on Article 10, paragraph 25 of the Commentary on Article 11 and paragraph 21 of the Commentary on Article 12, potential abuses may result from the transfer of shares, debt-claims, rights or property to permanent establishments set up solely for that purpose in countries that do not tax such investment income or offer preferential treatment to the income from such assets. Where the State of residence exempts the investment income of such permanent establishments situated in third States, the State of source should not be expected to grant treaty***

benefits with respect to such income. The proposed paragraph, which applies where a Contracting State exempts the investment income of enterprises of that State that are attributable to permanent establishments situated in a third State, provides that treaty benefits will not be granted in such cases. That rule does not apply to profits that are derived in connection with, or that are incidental to, the active conduct of a business through the permanent establishment, excluding an investment business that is not carried by a bank, insurance enterprise or securities dealer; it also does not apply if the income received from the State of source constitutes royalties received as compensation for the use of, or the right to use, intangible property produced or developed by the enterprise through the permanent establishment.

2. In any case where benefits are denied under this paragraph, the enterprise that derives the relevant income should have access to the discretionary relief provision of paragraph 5 of Article [X] in order to ensure that benefits may be granted where the establishment, acquisition or maintenance of the permanent establishment and the conduct of its operations did not have as one of its principal purposes the obtaining of benefits under this Convention. This result could be achieved by including this provision into Article [X].

3. Some States may prefer a more comprehensive solution that would not be restricted to situations where an enterprise of a Contracting State is exempt, in that State, on the profits attributable to a permanent establishment situated in a third State. In such a case, the provision would be applicable in any case where income derived from one Contracting State that is attributable to a permanent establishment situated in a third State is subject to combined taxation, in the State of the enterprise and the State of the permanent establishment, at an effective rate that is less than the 60 per cent threshold. The following is an example of a provision that could be used for that purpose:

> ***Notwithstanding the other provisions of this Convention, where an enterprise of a Contracting State derives income from the other Contracting State and that income is attributable to a permanent establishment of that enterprise that is situated in a third State, the tax benefits that would otherwise apply under the other provisions of this Convention will not apply to that income if the profits of that permanent establishment are subject to a combined aggregate effective rate of tax in the first-mentioned Contracting State and third State that is less than 60 percent of the general rate of company tax applicable in the first-mentioned Contracting State. Any dividends, interest or royalties to which the provisions of this paragraph apply shall remain taxable in the other Contracting State at a rate that shall not exceed 15 percent of the gross amount thereof. Any other income to which the provisions of this paragraph apply shall remain taxable according to the laws of the other Contracting State notwithstanding any other provision of this Convention. The provisions of this paragraph shall not apply if:***
>
> ***a) in the case of royalties, the royalties are received as compensation for the use of, or the right to use, intangible property produced or developed by the enterprise through the permanent establishment; or***
>
> ***b) in the case of any other income, the income derived from the other Contracting State is derived in connection with, or is incidental to, the active conduct of a business carried on in the third State through***

the permanent establishment (other than the business of making, managing or simply holding investments for the enterprise's own account, unless these activities are banking, insurance or securities activities carried on by a bank, insurance enterprise or registered securities dealer, respectively).]

2. Cases where a person tries to abuse the provisions of domestic tax law using treaty benefits

53. Many tax avoidance risks that threaten the tax base are not caused by tax treaties but may be facilitated by treaties. In these cases, it is not sufficient to address the treaty issues: changes to domestic law are also required. Avoidance strategies that fall into this category include:

- Thin capitalisation and other financing transactions that use tax deductions to lower borrowing costs;
- Dual residence strategies (e.g. a company is resident for domestic tax purposes but non-resident for treaty purposes);
- Transfer mispricing;
- Arbitrage transactions that take advantage of mismatches found in the domestic law of one State and that are
    - related to the characterisation of income (e.g. by transforming business profits into capital gain) or payments (e.g. by transforming dividends into interest);
    - related to the treatment of taxpayers (e.g. by transferring income to tax-exempt entities or entities that have accumulated tax losses; by transferring income from non-residents to residents);
    - related to timing differences (e.g. by delaying taxation or advancing deductions).
- Arbitrage transactions that take advantage of mismatches between the domestic laws of two States and that are
    - related to the characterisation of income;
    - related to the characterisation of entities;
    - related to timing differences.
- Transactions that abuse relief of double taxation mechanisms (by producing income that is not taxable in the State of source but must be exempted by the State of residence or by abusing foreign tax credit mechanisms).

54. The work on other aspects of the Action Plan, in particular Action 2 (Neutralise the effects of hybrid mismatch arrangements), Action 3 (Strengthen CFC rules), Action 4 (Limit base erosion via interest deductions and other financial payments) and Actions 8, 9 and 10 dealing with Transfer Pricing has addressed many of these transactions. The main objective of the work aimed at preventing the granting of treaty benefits with respect to these transactions is to ensure that treaties do not prevent the application of specific domestic law provisions that would prevent these transactions.[15] Granting the benefits of these treaty provisions in such cases would be inappropriate to the extent that the result would be the avoidance of domestic tax. Such cases include situations where it is argued that

- Provisions of a tax treaty prevent the application of a domestic GAAR;
- Article 24(4) and Article 24(5) prevent the application of domestic thin-capitalisation rules;

- Article 7 and/or Article 10(5) prevent the application of CFC rules;
- Article 13(5) prevents the application of exit or departure taxes;
- Article 24(5) prevents the application of domestic rules that restrict tax consolidation to resident entities;
- Article 13(5) prevents the application of dividend stripping rules targeted at transactions designed to transform dividends into treaty-exempt capital gains;
- Article 13(5) prevents the application of domestic assignment of income rules (such as grantor trust rules).

55. The Commentary on the Articles of the OECD Model already addresses a number of these issues. For instance, it deals expressly with CFC rules (paragraph 23 of the Commentary on Article 1 provides that treaties do not prevent the application of such rules). It also refers to thin capitalisation rules (paragraph 3 of the Commentary on Article 9 suggests that treaties do not prevent the application of such rules "insofar as their effect is to assimilate the profits of the borrower to an amount corresponding to the profits which would have accrued in an arm's length situation"). It does not, however, address a number of other specific domestic anti-abuse rules.

56. Paragraphs 22 and 22.1 of the Commentary on Article 1 provide a more general discussion of the interaction between tax treaties and domestic anti-abuse rules. These paragraphs conclude that a conflict would not occur in the case of the application of certain domestic anti-abuse rules to a transaction that constitutes an abuse of the tax treaty:

> 22. Other forms of abuse of tax treaties (e.g. the use of a base company) and possible ways to deal with them, including "substance-over-form", "economic substance" and general anti-abuse rules have also been analysed, particularly as concerns the question of whether these rules conflict with tax treaties [...]
>
> 22.1 Such rules are part of the basic domestic rules set by domestic tax laws for determining which facts give rise to a tax liability; these rules are not addressed in tax treaties and are therefore not affected by them. Thus, as a general rule and having regard to paragraph 9.5, there will be no conflict. [...]

57. Paragraph 9.5 of the Commentary on Article 1 offers the following guidance as to what constitutes an abuse of the provisions of a tax treaty:

> A guiding principle is that the benefits of a double taxation convention should not be available where a main purpose for entering into certain transactions or arrangements was to secure a more favourable tax position and obtaining that more favourable treatment in these circumstances would be contrary to the object and purpose of the relevant provisions.

58. As indicated in subsection A.1, a new general anti-abuse rule that will incorporate the principle already recognised in paragraph 9.5 of the Commentary on Article 1 will be included in the OECD Model. The incorporation of that principle into tax treaties will provide a clear statement that the Contracting States want to deny the application of the provisions of their treaty when transactions or arrangements are entered into in order to obtain the benefits of these provisions in inappropriate circumstances. The incorporation of that principle into a specific treaty provision does not modify, however, the conclusions already reflected in the Commentary on Article 1 concerning the interaction between treaties and domestic anti-abuse rules; such conclusions remain applicable, in particular with respect to treaties that do not incorporate the new general anti-abuse rule.

59. The following revised version of the section on "Improper use of the Convention" currently found in the Commentary on Article 1 will reflect that conclusion and will better articulate the relationship between domestic anti-abuse rules and tax treaties:

Improper use of the Convention

7. The principal purpose of double taxation conventions is to promote, by eliminating international double taxation, exchanges of goods and services, and the movement of capital and persons. As confirmed in the preamble of the Convention, it is also part of the purposes of tax conventions to prevent tax avoidance and evasion.

8. The extension of the network of tax conventions increases the risk of abuse by facilitating the use of arrangements aimed at securing the benefits of both the tax advantages available under certain domestic laws and the reliefs from tax provided for in these conventions.

9. This would be the case, for example, if a person (whether or not a resident of a Contracting State), acts through a legal entity created in a State essentially to obtain treaty benefits that would not be available directly. Another case would be an individual who has in a Contracting State both his permanent home and all his economic interests, including a substantial shareholding in a company of that State, and who, essentially in order to sell the shares and escape taxation in that State on the capital gains from the alienation (by virtue of paragraph 5 of Article 13), transfers his permanent home to the other Contracting State, where such gains are subject to little or no tax.

Addressing tax avoidance through tax conventions

10. Paragraph 7 of Article [***X***] [***the PPT rule***] ***and the specific treaty anti-abuse rules included in tax conventions are aimed at these and other transactions and arrangements entered into for the purpose of obtaining treaty benefits in inappropriate circumstances.*** [***rest of previous paragraph 1 has been moved to paragraph 19***] ***Where, however, a tax convention does not include such rules, the question may arise whether the benefits of the tax convention should be granted when transactions that constitute an abuse of the provisions of that convention are entered into.***

11. Many States address that question by taking account of the fact that taxes are ultimately imposed through the provisions of domestic law, as restricted (and in some rare cases, broadened) by the provisions of tax conventions. Thus, any abuse of the provisions of a tax convention could also be characterised as an abuse of the provisions of domestic law under which tax will be levied. For these States, the issue then becomes whether the provisions of tax conventions may prevent the application of the anti-abuse provisions of domestic law, which is the question addressed in paragraphs 19 to 26.8 below. As explained in these paragraphs, as a general rule, there will be no conflict between such rules and the provisions of tax conventions.

12. Other States prefer to view some abuses as being abuses of the convention itself, as opposed to abuses of domestic law. These States, however, then consider that a proper construction of tax conventions allows them to disregard abusive transactions, such as those entered into with the view to obtaining unintended benefits under the provisions of these conventions. This interpretation results from

the object and purpose of tax conventions as well as the obligation to interpret them in good faith (see Article 31 of the Vienna Convention on the Law of Treaties).

13. Under both approaches, therefore, it is agreed that States do not have to grant the benefits of a double taxation convention where arrangements that constitute an abuse of the provisions of the convention have been entered into.

14. It is important to note, however, that it should not be lightly assumed that a taxpayer is entering into the type of abusive transactions referred to above. A guiding principle is that the benefits of a double taxation convention should not be available where a main purpose for entering into certain transactions or arrangements was to secure a more favourable tax position and obtaining that more favourable treatment in these circumstances would be contrary to the object and purpose of the relevant provisions. That principle applies independently from the provisions of paragraph 7 of Article [X] [*the PPT rule*]*, which merely confirm it.*

15. The potential application of these principles or of paragraph 7 of Article [X] *does not mean that there is no need for the inclusion, in tax conventions, of specific provisions aimed at preventing particular forms of tax avoidance. Where specific avoidance techniques have been identified or where the use of such techniques is especially problematic, it will often be useful to add to the Convention provisions that focus directly on the relevant avoidance strategy. Also, this will be necessary where a State which adopts the view described in paragraph 11 above believes that its domestic law lacks the anti-avoidance rules or principles necessary to properly address such strategy.*

16. For instance, some forms of tax avoidance have already been expressly dealt with in the Convention, e.g. by the introduction of the concept of "beneficial owner" (in Articles 10, 11, and 12) and of special provisions such as paragraph 2 of Article 17 dealing with so-called artiste-companies. Such problems are also mentioned in the Commentaries on Article 10 (paragraphs 17 and 22), Article 11 (paragraph 12) and Article 12 (paragraph 7).

17. Also, in some cases, claims to treaty benefits by subsidiary companies, in particular companies established in tax havens or benefiting from harmful preferential regimes, may be refused where careful consideration of the facts and circumstances of a case shows that the place of effective management of a subsidiary does not lie in its alleged state of residence but, rather, lies in the state of residence of the parent company so as to make it a resident of that latter state for domestic law purposes (this will be relevant where the domestic law of a state uses the place of management of a legal person, or a similar criterion, to determine its residence).

18. Careful consideration of the facts and circumstances of a case may also show that a subsidiary was managed in the state of residence of its parent in such a way that the subsidiary had a permanent establishment (e.g. by having a place of management) in that state to which all or a substantial part of its profits were properly attributable.

Addressing tax avoidance through domestic anti-abuse rules and judicial doctrines

19. Domestic anti-abuse rules and judicial doctrines may also be used to address transactions and arrangements entered into for the purpose of obtaining treaty benefits in inappropriate circumstances. These rules and doctrines may also address situations where transactions or arrangements are entered into for the purpose of abusing both domestic laws and tax conventions.

20. For these reasons, domestic anti-abuse rules and judicial doctrines play an important role in preventing treaty benefits from being granted in inappropriate circumstances. The application of such domestic anti-abuse rules and doctrines, however, raises the issue of possible conflicts with treaty provisions, in particular where treaty provisions are relied upon in order to facilitate the abuse of domestic law provisions (e.g. where it is claimed that treaty provisions protect the taxpayer from the application of certain domestic anti-abuse rules). This issue is discussed below in relation to specific legislative anti-abuse rules, general legislative anti-abuse rules and judicial doctrines.

Specific legislative anti-abuse rules

21. Tax authorities seeking to address the improper use of a tax treaty may first consider the application of specific anti-abuse rules included in their domestic tax law.

22. Many specific anti-abuse rules found in domestic law apply primarily in cross-border situations and may be relevant for the application of tax treaties. For instance, thin capitalisation rules may apply to restrict the deduction of base-eroding interest payments to residents of treaty countries; transfer pricing rules (even if not designed primarily as anti-abuse rules) may prevent the artificial shifting of income from a resident enterprise to an enterprise that is resident of a treaty country; exit or departure tax rules may prevent the avoidance of capital gains tax through a change of residence before the realisation of a treaty-exempt capital gain; dividend stripping rules may prevent the avoidance of domestic dividend withholding taxes through transactions designed to transform dividends into treaty-exempt capital gains; and anti-conduit rules may prevent certain avoidance transactions involving the use of conduit arrangements.

23. Generally, where the application of provisions of domestic law and of those of tax treaties produces conflicting results, the provisions of tax treaties are intended to prevail. This is a logical consequence of the principle of "pacta sunt servanda" which is incorporated in Article 26 of the Vienna Convention on the Law of Treaties. Thus, if the application of specific anti-abuse rules found in domestic law were to result in a tax treatment that is not in accordance with the provisions of a tax treaty, this would conflict with the provisions of that treaty and the provisions of the treaty should prevail under public international law.[1]

[Footnote to paragraph 23:] 1. Under Article 60 of the Vienna Convention on the Law of Treaties "[a] material breach of a bilateral treaty by one of the parties entitles the other to invoke the breach as a ground for terminating the treaty or suspending its operation in whole or in part".

24. As explained below, however, such conflicts will often be avoided and each case must be analysed based on its own circumstances.

25. First, a treaty may specifically allow the application of certain types of specific domestic anti-abuse rules. For example, Article 9 specifically authorises the application of domestic rules in the circumstances defined by that Article. Also, many treaties include specific provisions clarifying that there is no conflict or, even if there is a conflict, allowing the application of the domestic rules.

This would be the case, for example, for a treaty rule that expressly allows the application of a thin capitalisation rule found in the domestic law of one or both Contracting States.

26. Second, many provisions of the Convention depend on the application of domestic law. This is the case, for instance, for the determination of the residence of a person (see paragraph 1 of Article 4), the determination of what is immovable property (see paragraph 2 of Article 6) and the determination of when income from corporate rights might be treated as a dividend (see paragraph 3 of Article 10). More generally, paragraph 2 of Article 3 makes domestic rules relevant for the purposes of determining the meaning of terms that are not defined in the Convention. In many cases, therefore, the application of specific anti-abuse rules found in domestic law will have an impact on how the treaty provisions are applied rather than produce conflicting results. This would be the case, for example, if a domestic law provision treats the profits realised by a shareholder when a company redeems some of its shares as dividends: although such a redemption could be considered to constitute an alienation for the purposes of paragraph 5 of Article 13, paragraph 28 of the Commentary on Article 10 recognises that such profits will constitute dividends for the purposes of Article 10 if the profits are treated as dividends under domestic law.

26.1 Third, the application of tax treaty provisions in a case that involves an abuse of these provisions may be denied under paragraph 7 of Article [X] [the PPT rule] or, in the case of a treaty that does not include that paragraph, under the principles put forward in paragraphs 13 and 14 above. In such a case, there will be no conflict with the treaty provisions if the benefits of the treaty are denied under both paragraph 7 of Article [X] (or the principles in paragraphs 13 and 14 above) and the relevant domestic specific anti-abuse rules. Domestic specific anti-abuse rules, however, are often drafted with reference to objective facts, such as the existence of a certain level of shareholding or a certain debt-equity ratio. Whilst this facilitates their application and provides greater certainty, it may sometimes result in the application of such a rule in a case where the rule conflicts with a provision of the Convention and where paragraph 7 does not apply to deny the benefits of that provision (and where the principles of paragraphs 13-14 above also do not apply). In such a case, the Convention will not allow the application of the domestic rule to the extent of the conflict. An example of such a case would be where a domestic law rule that State A adopted to prevent temporary changes of residence for tax purposes would provide for the taxation of an individual who is a resident of State B on gains from the alienation of property situated in a third State if that individual was a resident of State A when the property was acquired and was a resident of State A for at least seven of the 10 years preceding the alienation. In such a case, to the extent that paragraph 5 of Article 13 would prevent the taxation of that individual by State A upon the alienation of the property, the Convention would prevent the application of that domestic rule unless the benefits of paragraph 5 of Article 13 could be denied, in that specific case, under paragraph 7 or the principles in paragraphs 13-14 above.

26.2 Fourth, the application of tax treaty provisions may be denied under judicial doctrines or principles applicable to the interpretation of the treaty (see paragraph 26.5 below). In such a case, there will be no conflict with the treaty provisions if the benefits of the treaty are denied under both a proper interpretation of the treaty and as result of the application of domestic specific anti-abuse rules. Assume, for example, that the domestic law of State A provides for the taxation of gains derived from the alienation of shares of a domestic company in which the alienator holds more than 25 per cent of the capital if that alienator was a resident of State A for at least seven of the 10 years preceding the alienation. In year 2, an individual who was a resident of State A for the previous 10 years becomes a resident of State B. Shortly after becoming a resident of State B, the individual sells the totality of the shares of a small company that he previously established in State A. The facts reveal, however, that all the elements of the sale were finalised in year 1, that an interest-free "loan" corresponding to the sale price was made by the purchaser to the seller at that time, that the purchaser cancelled the loan when the shares were sold to the purchaser in year 2 and that the purchaser exercised de facto control of the company from year 1. Although the gain from the sale of the shares might otherwise fall under paragraph 5 of Article 13 of the State A-State B treaty, the circumstances of the transfer of the shares are such that the alienation in year 2 constitutes a sham within the meaning given to that term by the courts of State A. In that case, to the extent that the sham transaction doctrine developed by the courts of State A does not conflict with the rules of interpretation of treaties, it will be possible to apply that doctrine when interpreting paragraph 5 of Article 13 of the State A-State B treaty, which will allow State A to tax the relevant gain under its domestic law rule.

General legislative anti-abuse rules

26.3 Many countries have included in their domestic law a legislative anti-abuse rule of general application intended to prevent abusive arrangements that are not adequately dealt with through specific anti-abuse rules or judicial doctrines.

26.4 The application of such general anti-abuse rules also raises the question of a possible conflict with the provisions of a tax treaty. In the vast majority of cases, however, no such conflict will arise. Conflicts will first be avoided for reasons similar to those presented in paragraphs 25 and 26 above. In addition, where the main aspects of these domestic general anti-abuse rules are in conformity with the principle of paragraph 14 above and are therefore similar to the main aspects of paragraph 7 of Article [X], which incorporates this guiding principle, it is clear that no conflict will be possible since the relevant domestic general anti-abuse rule will apply in the same circumstances in which the benefits of the Convention would be denied under paragraph 7, or, in the case of a treaty that does not include that paragraph, to the guiding principle in paragraph 14 above.

Judicial doctrines that are part of domestic law

26.5 In the process of interpreting tax legislation in cases dealing with tax avoidance, the courts of many countries have developed a number of judicial doctrines or principles of interpretation. These include doctrines such as substance over form, economic substance, sham, business purpose, step-transaction, abuse of law and fraus legis. These doctrines and principles of interpretation, which vary from country to country and evolve over time based on refinements or changes resulting from subsequent court decisions, are essentially views expressed by courts as to how tax legislation should be interpreted. Whilst the interpretation of tax treaties is governed by general rules that have been codified in Articles 31 to 33 of the Vienna Convention on the Law of Treaties, these general rules do not prevent the application of similar judicial doctrines and principles to the interpretation of the provisions of tax treaties. If, for example, the courts of one country have determined that, as a matter of legal interpretation, domestic tax provisions should apply on the basis of the economic substance of certain transactions, there is nothing that prevents a similar approach from being adopted with respect to the application of the provisions of a tax treaty to similar transactions. This is illustrated by the example in paragraph 26.2 above.

26.6 As a general rule and having regard to paragraph 14, therefore, the preceding analysis leads to the conclusion that there will be no conflict between tax conventions and judicial anti-abuse doctrines or general domestic anti-abuse rules. For example, to the extent that the application of a general domestic anti-abuse rule or a judicial doctrine such as "substance over form" or "economic substance" results in a recharacterisation of income or in a redetermination of the taxpayer who is considered to derive such income, the provisions of the Convention will be applied taking into account these changes.

26.7 Whilst these rules do not conflict with tax conventions, there is agreement that member countries should carefully observe the specific obligations enshrined in tax treaties to relieve double taxation as long as there is no clear evidence that the treaties are being abused.

Controlled foreign company provisions

26.8 A significant number of countries have adopted controlled foreign company provisions to address issues related to the use of foreign base companies. Whilst the design of this type of legislation varies considerably among countries, a common feature of these rules, which are now internationally recognised as a legitimate instrument to protect the domestic tax base, is that they result in a Contracting State taxing its residents on income attributable to their participation in certain foreign entities. It has sometimes been argued, based on a certain interpretation of provisions of the Convention such as paragraph 1 of Article 7 and paragraph 5 of Article 10, that this common feature of controlled foreign company legislation conflicted with these provisions. Since such legislation results in a State taxing its own residents, paragraph 3 of Article 1 confirms that it does not conflict with tax conventions. The same conclusion must be reached in the case of conventions that do not include a provision similar to paragraph 3 of Article 1; for the reasons explained in paragraphs 14 of the Commentary on Article 7 and 37 of the Commentary on Article 10, the interpretation according to which these Articles would prevent the application of controlled foreign company provisions does not accord with the text of paragraph 1 of Article 7 and paragraph 5 of Article 10. It also does not hold when these provisions are read in their context. Thus, whilst some countries have felt it useful to expressly clarify, in their conventions, that controlled foreign companies legislation did not conflict with the Convention, such clarification is not necessary. It is recognised that controlled foreign company legislation structured in this way is not contrary to the provisions of the Convention.

60. Two specific issues related to the interaction between treaties and specific domestic anti-abuse rules are discussed below. The first issue deals with domestic anti-abuse rules found in the domestic law of one State that are aimed at preventing avoidance arrangements

entered into by residents of that State. The second issue, which is indirectly related to the first one, deals with the application of tax treaties to so-called departure or exit taxes.

a) Application of tax treaties to restrict a Contracting State's right to tax its own residents

61. The majority of the provisions included in tax treaties are intended to restrict the right of a Contracting State to tax the residents of the other Contracting State. In some limited cases, however, it has been argued that some provisions that are aimed at the taxation of non-residents could be interpreted as limiting a Contracting State's right to tax its own residents. Such interpretations have been rejected in paragraph 6.1 of the Commentary on Article 1, which deals with a Contracting State's right to tax partners who are its own residents on their share of the income of a partnership that is treated as a resident of the other Contracting State, as well as in paragraph 23 of the same Commentary, which addresses the case of controlled foreign companies rules (see also paragraph 14 of the Commentary on Article 7, which deals with the same issue).

62. It was concluded that the principle reflected in paragraph 6.1 of the Commentary on Article 1 should be applicable to the vast majority of the provisions of the Model Tax Convention in order to prevent interpretations intended to circumvent the application of a Contracting State's domestic anti-abuse rules (as illustrated by the example of controlled foreign companies rules). This corresponds to the practice long followed by the United States in its tax treaties, where a so-called "saving clause"[16] confirms the Contracting States' right to tax their residents (and citizens, in the case, of the United States) notwithstanding the provisions of the treaty except those, such as the rules on relief of double taxation, that are clearly intended to apply to residents.

63. The following changes will be made to the Model Tax Convention as a result of that decision:

Add the following paragraph 3 to Article 1:

> ***3. This Convention shall not affect the taxation, by a Contracting State, of its residents except with respect to the benefits granted under paragraph 3 of Article 7, paragraph 2 of Article 9 and Articles 19, 20, 23 A [23 B], 24 and 25 and 28.***

Add the following paragraphs 26.17 to 26.21 to the Commentary on Article 1 (other consequential changes to the Commentary would be required):

> ***26.17 Whilst some provisions of the Convention (e.g. Articles 23 A and 23 B) are clearly intended to affect how a Contracting State taxes its own residents, the object of the majority of the provisions of the Convention is to restrict the right of a Contracting State to tax the residents of the other Contracting State. In some limited cases, however, it has been argued that some provisions could be interpreted as limiting a Contracting State's right to tax its own residents in cases where this was not intended (see, for example, paragraph 23 above, which addresses the case of controlled foreign companies provisions).***
>
> ***26.18 Paragraph 3 confirms the general principle that the Convention does not restrict a Contracting State's right to tax its own residents except where this is intended and lists the provisions with respect to which that principle is not applicable.***

26.19 The exceptions so listed are intended to cover all cases where it is envisaged in the Convention that a Contracting State may have to provide treaty benefits to its own residents (whether or not these or similar benefits are provided under the domestic law of that State). These provisions are:

- *Paragraph 3 of Article 7, which requires a Contracting State to grant to an enterprise of that State a correlative adjustment following an initial adjustment made by the other Contracting State, in accordance with paragraph 2 of Article 7, to the amount of tax charged on the profits of a permanent establishment of the enterprise.*
- *Paragraph 2 of Article 9, which requires a Contracting State to grant to an enterprise of that State a corresponding adjustment following an initial adjustment made by the other Contracting State, in accordance with paragraph 1 of Article 9, to the amount of tax charged on the profits of an associated enterprise.*
- *Article 19, which may affect how a Contracting State taxes an individual who is resident of that State if that individual derives income in respect of services rendered to the other Contracting State or a political subdivision or local authority thereof.*
- *Article 20, which may affect how a Contracting State taxes an individual who is resident of that State if that individual is also a student who meets the conditions of that Article.*
- *Articles 23 A and 23 B, which require a Contracting State to provide relief of double taxation to its residents with respect to the income that the other State may tax in accordance with the Convention (including profits that are attributable to a permanent establishment situated in the other Contracting State in accordance with paragraph 2 of Article 7).*
- *Article 24, which protects residents of a Contracting State against certain discriminatory taxation practices by that State (such as rules that discriminate between two persons based on their nationality).*
- *Article 25, which allows residents of a Contracting State to request that the competent authority of that State consider cases of taxation not in accordance with the Convention.*
- *Article 28, which may affect how a Contracting State taxes an individual who is resident of that State when that individual is a member of the diplomatic mission or consular post of the other Contracting State.*

26.20 The list of exceptions included in paragraph 3 should include any other provision that the Contracting States may agree to include in their bilateral convention where it is intended that this provision should affect the taxation, by a Contracting State, of its own residents. For instance, if the Contracting States agree, in accordance with paragraph 27 of the Commentary on Article 18, to include in their bilateral convention a provision according to which pensions and other payments made under the social security legislation of a Contracting State shall be taxable only in that State, they should include a reference to that provision in the list of exceptions included in paragraph 3.

26.21 The term "resident", as used in paragraph 3 and throughout the Convention, is defined in Article 4. Where, under paragraph 1 of Article 4, a person is considered to be a resident of both Contracting States based on the domestic laws of these States, paragraphs 2 and 3 of that Article determine a single State of residence for the purposes of the Convention. Thus, paragraph 3 does not apply to an individual or legal person who is a resident of one of the Contracting States under the laws of that State but who, for the purposes of the Convention, is deemed to be a resident only of the other Contracting State.

64. During the work on the above new provision, a number of issues related to relief of double taxation were discussed. It was agreed that, as a matter of principle, Articles 23 A and 23 B of the OECD Model only required a Contracting State to relieve double taxation when income was taxable in the other State under treaty provisions allowing that other State to tax the relevant income as the State of source or as a State where there is a permanent establishment to which that income is attributable. The following draft proposal for changes to Articles 23 A and 23 B was put forward during the last stages of that work in order to confirm that principle. It is intended to finalise the work on that draft proposal in the first part of 2016, which will allow changes that could result from that work to be considered as part of the negotiation of the multilateral instrument that will implement the results of the work on treaty issues mandated by the BEPS Action Plan:

Replace paragraph 1 of Article 23 A as follows:

1. Where a resident of a Contracting State derives income or owns capital which ***may be taxed in the other Contracting State*** in accordance with the provisions of this Convention ***(except to the extent that these provisions allow taxation by that other State solely because the income is also income derived by a resident of that State)***, ~~may be taxed in the other Contracting State,~~ the first-mentioned State shall, subject to the provisions of paragraphs 2 and 3, exempt such income or capital from tax.

Replace paragraph 1 of Article 23 B as follows:

1. Where a resident of a Contracting State derives income or owns capital which ***may be taxed in the other Contracting State*** in accordance with the provisions of this Convention ***(except to the extent that these provisions allow taxation by that other State solely because the income is also income derived by a resident of that State)***, ~~may be taxed in the other Contracting State~~, the first-mentioned State shall allow:

a) as a deduction from the tax on the income of that resident, an amount equal to the income tax paid in that other State;

b) as a deduction from the tax on the capital of that resident, an amount equal to the capital tax paid in that other State.

Such deduction in either case shall not, however, exceed that part of the income tax or capital tax, as computed before the deduction is given, which is attributable, as the case may be, to the income or the capital which may be taxed in that other State.

Add the following paragraph 11.1 to the Commentary on Articles 23 A and 23 B (other consequential changes to the Commentary may be required):

11.1 In some cases, the same income or capital may be taxed by each Contracting State as income or capital of one of its residents. This may happen where, for example, one of the Contracting States taxes the worldwide income of an entity that is a resident of that State whereas the other State views that entity as fiscally transparent and taxes the members of that entity who are residents of that other State on their respective share of the income. The phrase "(except to the extent that these provisions allow taxation by that other State solely because the income is also income derived by a resident of that State)" clarifies that in such cases, both States are not reciprocally obliged to provide relief for each other's tax levied exclusively on the basis of the residence of the taxpayer and that each State is therefore only obliged to provide relief of double taxation to the extent that taxation by the other State is in accordance with provisions of the Convention that allow taxation of the relevant income as the State of source or as a State where there is a permanent establishment to which that income is attributable, thereby excluding taxation that would solely be in accordance with paragraph 3 of Article 1. Whilst this result would logically follow from the wording of Articles 23 A and 23 B even in the absence of that phrase, the addition of the phrase removes any doubt in this respect.

b) Departure or exit taxes

65. In a number of States, liability to tax on some types of income that have accrued for the benefit of a resident (whether an individual or a legal person) is triggered in the event that the resident ceases to be a resident of that State. Taxes levied in these circumstances are generally referred to as "departure taxes" or "exit taxes" and may apply, for example, to accrued pension rights and accrued capital gains.

66. To the extent that the liability to such a tax arises when a person is still a resident of the State that applies the tax and does not extend to income accruing after the cessation of residence, nothing in the Convention, and in particular in Articles 13 and 18, prevents the application of that form of taxation. Thus, tax treaties do not prevent the application of domestic tax rules according to which a person is considered to have realised pension income, or to have alienated property for capital gain tax purposes, immediately before ceasing to be a resident. The provisions of tax treaties do not govern when income is realised for domestic tax purposes (see, for example, paragraphs 3 and 7 to 9 of the Commentary on Article 13); also, since the provisions of tax treaties apply regardless of when tax is actually paid (see, for example, paragraph 12.1 of the Commentary on Article 15), it does not matter when such taxes become payable, The application of such taxes, however, creates risks of double taxation where the relevant person becomes a resident of another State which seeks to tax the same income at a different time, e.g. when pension income is actually received or when assets are sold to third parties. This problem, which is the result of that person being a resident of two States at different times and of these States levying tax upon the realisation of different events, is discussed in paragraphs 4.1 to 4.3 of the Commentary on Article 23 A and 23 B. As indicated in paragraph 4.3 of that Commentary, which addresses a similar example where two States of residence tax the benefit arising from an employee stock-option at different times:

> The mutual agreement procedure could be used to deal with such a case. One possible basis to solve the case would be for the competent authorities of the two

States to agree that each State should provide relief as regards the residence-based tax that was levied by the other State on the part of the benefit that relates to services rendered during the period while the employee was a resident of that other State.

67. Based on that approach, a possible basis for solving double taxation situations arising from the application of departure taxes would be for the competent authorities of the two States involved to agree, through the mutual agreement procedure, that each State should provide relief as regards the residence-based tax that was levied by the other State on the part of the income that accrued while the person was a resident of that other State. This would mean that the new State of residence would provide relief for the departure tax levied by the previous State of residence on income that accrued whilst the person was a resident of that other State, except to the extent that the new State of residence would have had source taxation rights at the time that income was taxed (i.e. as a result of paragraphs 2 or 4 of Article 13). States wishing to provide expressly for that result in their tax treaties are free to include provisions to that effect.

B. Clarification that tax treaties are not intended to be used to generate double non-taxation

68. The second part of the work mandated by Action 6 was to "clarify that tax treaties are not intended to be used to generate double non-taxation".

69. The existing provisions of tax treaties were developed with the prime objective of preventing double-taxation. This was reflected in the title proposed in both the 1963 Draft Double Taxation Convention on Income and Capital and the 1977 Model Double Taxation Convention on Income and Capital, which was:

> Convention between (State A) and (State B) for the avoidance of double taxation with respect to taxes on income and on capital

70. In 1977, however, the Commentary on Article 1 was modified to provide expressly that tax treaties were no intended to encourage tax avoidance or evasion. The relevant part of paragraph 7 of the Commentary read as follows:

> The purpose of double taxation conventions is to promote, by eliminating international double taxation, exchanges of goods and services, and the movement of capital and persons; they should not, however, help tax avoidance or evasion.

71. In 2003, that paragraph was amended to clarify that the prevention of tax avoidance was also a purpose of tax treaties. Paragraph 7 now reads as follows:

> The principal purpose of double taxation conventions is to promote, by eliminating international double taxation, exchanges of goods and services, and the movement of capital and persons. It is also a purpose of tax conventions to prevent tax avoidance and evasion.

72. In order to provide the clarification required by Action 6, it has been decided to state clearly, in the title recommended by the OECD Model Tax Convention, that the prevention of tax evasion and avoidance is a purpose of tax treaties. It has also been decided that the OECD Model Tax Convention should recommend a preamble that provides expressly that States that enter into a tax treaty intend to eliminate double taxation without creating opportunities for tax evasion and avoidance. Given the particular concerns arising from treaty shopping arrangements, it has also been decided to refer expressly to such arrangements as one example of tax avoidance that should not result from tax treaties. The following are the changes that will be made to the OECD Model Tax Convention as a result of the work on this aspect of Action 6:

Replace the Title of the Convention (including its footnote) by the following:

> ***Convention between (State A) and (State B) for the elimination of double taxation with respect to taxes on income and on capital and the prevention of tax evasion and avoidance***~~Convention between (State A) and (State B) with respect to taxes on income and on capital1~~
>
> > ~~1. States wishing to do so may follow the widespread practice of including in the title a reference to either the avoidance of double taxation or to both the avoidance of double taxation and the prevention of fiscal evasion.~~

Replace the heading "Preamble to the Convention" (including its footnote) by the following:

~~PREAMBLE TO THE CONVENTION1~~

~~1. The Preamble of the Convention shall be drafted in accordance with the constitutional procedure of both Contracting States.~~

PREAMBLE TO THE CONVENTION

(State A) and (State B),

Desiring to further develop their economic relationship and to enhance their co-operation in tax matters,

Intending to conclude a Convention for the elimination of double taxation with respect to taxes on income and on capital without creating opportunities for non-taxation or reduced taxation through tax evasion or avoidance (including through treaty-shopping arrangements aimed at obtaining reliefs provided in this Convention for the indirect benefit of residents of third States)

Have agreed as follows:

73. The clear statement of the intention of the signatories to a tax treaty that appears in the above preamble will be relevant to the interpretation and application of the provisions of that treaty. According to the basic rule of interpretation of treaties in Article 31(1) of the *Vienna Convention on the Law of Treaties* (VCLT), "[a] treaty shall be interpreted in good faith in accordance with the ordinary meaning to be given to the terms of the treaty ***in their context*** and in the light of ***its object and purpose***" [emphasis added]. Article 31(2)[17] VCLT confirms that, for the purpose of this basic rule, the context of the treaty includes its preamble.[18]

74. The above changes to the Title and Preamble will be supplemented by the following changes to the Introduction to the OECD Model Tax Convention:

Replace paragraphs 2 and 3 of the Introduction by the following:

2. It has long been recognised among the member countries of the Organisation for Economic Co-operation and Development that it is desirable to clarify, standardise, and confirm the fiscal situation of taxpayers who are engaged in commercial, industrial, financial, or any other activities in other countries through the application by all countries of common solutions to identical cases of double taxation. ***These countries have also long recognised the need to improve administrative co-operation in tax matters, notably through exchange of information and assistance in collection of taxes, for the purpose of preventing tax evasion and avoidance.***

3. ***These are*** ~~this is~~ the main purpose*s* of the OECD Model Tax Convention on Income and on Capital, which provides a means of settling on a uniform basis the most common problems that arise in the field of international juridical double taxation. As recommended by the Council of the OECD,[1] member countries, when concluding or revising bilateral conventions, should conform to this Model Convention as interpreted by the Commentaries thereon and having regard to the reservations contained therein and their tax authorities should follow these Commentaries, as modified from time to time and subject to their observations thereon, when applying and interpreting the provisions of their bilateral tax conventions that are based on the Model Convention.

[*Footnote to paragraph 3*] 1. See Annex.

Replace paragraph 16 of the Introduction by the following:

16. In both the 1963 Draft Convention and the 1977 Model Convention, the title of the Model Convention included a reference to the elimination of double taxation. In recognition of the fact that the Model Convention does not deal exclusively with the elimination of double taxation but also addresses other issues, such as the prevention of tax evasion and ***avoidance as well as*** non-discrimination, it was ~~subsequently~~ decided, ***in 1992,*** to use a shorter title which did not include this reference. This change ~~has been~~ ***was*** made both on the cover page of this publication and in the Model Convention itself. However, it ~~is~~ ***was*** understood that the practice of many member countries ~~is~~ ***was*** still to include in the title a reference to either the elimination of double taxation or to both the elimination of double taxation and the prevention of fiscal evasion ***since both approaches emphasised these important purposes of the Convention.***

16.1 As a result of work undertaken as part of the OECD Action Plan on Base Erosion and Profit Shifting, in [***year***] ***the Committee decided to amend the title of the Convention and to include a preamble. The changes made expressly recognise that the purposes of the Convention are not limited to the elimination of double taxation and that the Contracting States do not intend the provisions of the Convention to create opportunities for non-taxation or reduced taxation through tax evasion and avoidance. Given the particular base erosion and profit shifting concerns arising from treaty-shopping arrangements, it was also decided to refer expressly to such arrangements as one example of tax avoidance that should not result from tax treaties, it being understood that this was only one example of tax avoidance that the Contracting States intend to prevent.***

16.2 Since the title and preamble form part of the context of the Convention[1] ***and constitute a general statement of the object and purpose of the Convention, they should play an important role in the interpretation of the provisions of the Convention. According to the general rule of treaty interpretation contained in Article 31(1) of the Vienna Convention on the Law of Treaties, "***[***a***] ***treaty shall be interpreted in good faith in accordance with the ordinary meaning to be given to the terms of the treaty in their context and in the light of its object and purpose."***

[***Footnote to paragraph 16.2:***] ***1. See Art. 31(2) VCLT.***

C. Tax policy considerations that, in general, countries should consider before deciding to enter into a tax treaty with another country

75. The third part of the work mandated by Action 6 was "to identify the tax policy considerations that, in general, countries should consider before deciding to enter into a tax treaty with another country".

76. It was agreed that having a clearer articulation of the policy considerations that, in general, countries should consider before deciding to enter into a tax treaty could make it easier for countries to justify their decisions not to enter into tax treaties with certain low or no-tax jurisdictions. It was also recognised, however, that there are also many non-tax factors that can lead to the conclusion of a tax treaty and that each country has a sovereign right to decide to enter into tax treaties with any jurisdiction with which it decides to do so.

77. In the course of the work on this aspect of Action 6, it was decided that the results of that work should reflect the fact that many of the tax policy considerations relevant to the conclusion of a tax treaty are also relevant to the question of whether to modify (or, ultimately, terminate) a treaty previously concluded in the event that a change of circumstances (such as changes to the domestic law of a treaty partner) raises BEPS concerns related to that treaty.

78. The following changes will be made to the Introduction of the OECD Model Tax Convention as a result of the work on this aspect of Action 6:

Insert the following paragraphs and new heading immediately after paragraph 15 in the Introduction to the OECD Model Convention (existing section C of the Introduction would become section D):

C. Tax policy considerations that are relevant to the decision of whether to enter into a tax treaty or amend an existing treaty

15.1 In 1997, the OECD Council adopted a recommendation that the Governments of member countries pursue their efforts to conclude bilateral tax treaties with those member countries, and where appropriate with non-member countries, with which they had not yet entered into such conventions. Whilst the question of whether or not to enter into a tax treaty with another country is for each State to decide on the basis of different factors, which include both tax and non-tax considerations, tax policy considerations will generally play a key role in that decision. The following paragraphs describe some of these tax policy considerations, which are relevant not only to the question of whether a treaty should be concluded with a State but also to the question of whether a State should seek to modify or replace an existing treaty or even, as a last resort, terminate a treaty (taking into account the fact that termination of a treaty often has a negative impact on large number of taxpayers who are not concerned by the situations that result in the termination of the treaty).

15.2 Since a main objective of tax treaties is the avoidance of double taxation in order to reduce tax obstacles to cross-border services, trade and investment,

the existence of risks of double taxation resulting from the interaction of the tax systems of the two States involved will be the primary tax policy concern. Such risks of double taxation will generally be more important where there is a significant level of existing or projected cross-border trade and investment between two States. Most of the provisions of tax treaties seek to alleviate double taxation by allocating taxing rights between the two States and it is assumed that where a State accepts treaty provisions that restrict its right to tax elements of income, it generally does so on the understanding that these elements of income are taxable in the other State. Where a State levies no or low income taxes, other States should consider whether there are risks of double taxation that would justify, by themselves, a tax treaty. States should also consider whether there are elements of another State's tax system that could increase the risk of non-taxation, which may include tax advantages that are ring-fenced from the domestic economy.

15.3 Accordingly, two States that consider entering into a tax treaty should evaluate the extent to which the risk of double taxation actually exists in cross-border situations involving their residents. A large number of cases of residence-source juridical double taxation can be eliminated through domestic provisions for the relief of double taxation (ordinarily in the form of either the exemption or credit method) which operate without the need for tax treaties. Whilst these domestic provisions will likely address most forms of residence-source juridical double taxation, they will not cover all cases of double taxation, especially if there are significant differences in the source rules of the two States or if the domestic law of these States does not allow for unilateral relief of economic double taxation (e.g. in the case of a transfer pricing adjustment made in another State).

15.4 Another tax policy consideration that is relevant to the conclusion of a tax treaty is the risk of excessive taxation that may result from high withholding taxes in the source State. Whilst mechanisms for the relief of double taxation will normally ensure that such high withholding taxes do not result in double taxation, to the extent that such taxes levied in the State of source exceed the amount of tax normally levied on profits in the State of residence, they may have a detrimental effect on cross-border trade and investment.

15.5 Further tax considerations that should be taken into account when considering entering into a tax treaty include the various features of tax treaties that encourage and foster economic ties between countries, such as the protection from discriminatory tax treatment of foreign investment that is offered by the non-discrimination rules of Article 24, the greater certainty of tax treatment for taxpayers who are entitled to benefit from the treaty and the fact that tax treaties provide, through the mutual agreement procedure, together with the possibility for Contracting States of moving to arbitration, a mechanism for the resolution of cross-border tax disputes.

15.6 An important objective of tax treaties being the prevention of tax avoidance and evasion, States should also consider whether their prospective treaty partners are willing and able to implement effectively the provisions of tax treaties concerning administrative assistance, such as the ability to exchange tax information, this being a key aspect that should be taken into account when deciding whether or not to enter into a tax treaty. The ability and willingness of

a State to provide assistance in the collection of taxes would also be a relevant factor to take into account. It should be noted, however, that in the absence of any actual risk of double taxation, these administrative provisions would not, by themselves, provide a sufficient tax policy basis for the existence of a tax treaty because such administrative assistance could be secured through more targeted alternative agreements, such as the conclusion of a tax information exchange agreement or the participation in the multilateral Convention on Mutual Administrative Assistance in Tax Matters.1

[***Footnote to paragraph 15.6:***] ***Available at*** www.oecd.org/ctp/exchange-of-tax-information/ENG-Amended-Convention.pdf

79. As already mentioned, many of the tax policy considerations relevant to the conclusion of a tax treaty are also relevant to the question of whether to modify (or, ultimately, terminate) a treaty previously concluded and certain changes to the domestic law of a treaty partner that are made after the conclusion of a tax treaty may raise BEPS concerns in relation to that treaty. In addition, when negotiating a tax treaty, a State may be concerned that certain features of the domestic law of the State with which it is negotiating may raise BEPS concerns even if these concerns may not be sufficient to justify not entering into a tax treaty with that State.

80. A State that has such BEPS concerns with respect to certain features of the domestic law of a prospective treaty partner or with respect to changes that might be made after the conclusion of a tax treaty may want to protect its tax base against such risks and may therefore find it useful to include in its treaties provisions that would restrict treaty benefits with respect to taxpayers that benefit from certain preferential tax rules or with respect to certain drastic changes that could be made to a country's domestic law after the conclusion of a treaty.

81. The following two proposals seek to achieve this objective. These proposals were first released for comments in May 2015. At about the same time, however, the United States released new versions of similar proposals[19] for public comments to be sent by 15 September 2015. When these new versions of the United States proposals were discussed, it was agreed that they should be further examined once finalised by the United States in the light of the comments that will be received on them. For that reason, the proposals below will need to be reviewed and, if necessary, finalised in the first part of 2016, which will allow any decision reached on these proposals to be taken into account as part of the negotiation of the multilateral instrument that will implement the results of the work on treaty issues mandated by the BEPS Action Plan. The following should therefore be considered as draft proposals to be further discussed:

[Proposal 1 – New treaty provisions on "special tax regimes"

New definition of "special tax regime" to be included in Article 3 (General Definitions)

X) … the term "special tax regime" with respect to an item of income or profit means any legislation, regulation or administrative practice that provides a preferential effective rate of taxation to such income or profit, including through reductions in the tax rate or the tax base. With regard to financing income, the term special tax regime includes notional interest deductions that are allowed without regard to liabilities for such interest. However, the term shall not include any legislation, regulation or administrative practice:

i) the application of which does not disproportionately benefit interest, royalties or other income, or any combination thereof;

ii) except with regard to financing income, that satisfies a substantial activity requirement;

iii) that is designed to prevent double taxation;

iv) that implements the principles of Article 7 (Business Profits) or Article 9 (Associated Enterprises);

v) that applies to persons which exclusively promote religious, charitable, scientific, artistic, cultural or educational activities;

vi) that applies to persons substantially all of the activity of which is to provide or administer pension or retirement benefits;

vii) that facilitates investment in widely-held entities that hold real property (immovable property), a diversified portfolio of securities, or any combination thereof, and that are subject to investor-protection regulation in the Contracting State in which the investment entity is established; or

viii) that the Contracting States have agreed shall not constitute a special tax regime because it does not result in a low effective rate of taxation;"

Protocol provisions

With reference to subparagraph X) of paragraph 1 of Article 3 (General Definitions):

The term "special tax regime" shall include:

a) in the case of _______:

i) [*list relevant specific legislation, regulations and/or administrative practices in the Contracting State*];

b) in the case of _______:

i) [*list relevant specific legislation, regulations and/or administrative practices in the Contracting State*].

With reference to subdivision *viii*) of subparagraph (X) of paragraph 1 of Article 3 (General Definitions):

The term "special tax regime" shall not include:

a) in the case of _______:

i) [*list relevant specific legislation, regulations and/or administrative practices in the Contracting State*];

b) in the case of _______:

i) [*list relevant specific legislation, regulations and/or administrative practices in the Contracting State*].

New Provisions for Articles 11, 12 and 21

New provision for Article 11 (Interest)

Interest arising in a Contracting State and beneficially owned by a resident of the other Contracting State may be taxed in the first-mentioned Contracting State in accordance with domestic law if such resident is subject to a special tax regime with respect to interest in its Contracting State of residence at any time during the taxable period in which the interest is paid.

New provision for Article 12 (Royalties)

Royalties arising in a Contracting State and beneficially owned by a resident of the other Contracting State may be taxed in the first-mentioned Contracting State in accordance with domestic law if such resident is subject to a special tax regime with respect to royalties in its Contracting State of residence at any time during the taxable period in which the royalties are paid.

New provision for Article 21 (Other income)

Other income arising in a Contracting State and beneficially owned by a resident of the other Contracting State may be taxed in the first-mentioned Contracting State in accordance with domestic law if such resident is subject to a special tax regime with respect to other income in its Contracting State of residence at any time during the taxable period in which the other income is paid.]

[Proposal 2 – New general treaty rule intended to make a tax treaty responsive to certain future changes in a country's domestic tax laws

1. If at any time after the signing of this Convention, either Contracting State provides an exemption from taxation to resident companies for substantially all foreign source income (including interest and royalties), the provisions of Articles 10 (Dividends), 11 (Interest), 12 (Royalties) and 21 (Other Income) may cease to have effect pursuant to paragraph 3 of this Article for payments to companies resident of either Contracting State.

2. If at any time after the signing of this Convention, either Contracting State provides an exemption from taxation to resident individuals for substantially all foreign source income (including interest and royalties), the provisions of Articles 10, 11, 12 and 21 may cease to have effect pursuant to paragraph 3 of this Article for payments to individuals resident of either Contracting State.

3. If the provisions of either paragraph 1 or paragraph 2 of this Article are satisfied, a Contracting State may notify the other Contracting State through diplomatic channels that it will cease to apply the provisions of Articles 10, 11, 12 and 21. In such case, the provisions of such Articles shall cease to have effect in both Contracting States with respect to payments to resident individuals or companies, as appropriate, six months after the date of such written notification, and the Contracting States shall consult with a view to concluding amendments to this Convention to restore the balance of benefits provided.]

Notes

1. See www.treasury.gov/press-center/press-releases/Pages/jl10057.aspx.

2. Cases where a resident of the Contracting State in which income originates seeks to obtain treaty benefits (e.g. through a transfer of residence to the other Contracting State or through the use of an entity established in that other State) could also be considered to constitute a form of treaty shopping and are addressed by the recommendations included in this report.

3. Reproduced at page R(5)-1 and R(6)-1 of the full version of the Model.

4. Reproduced at page R(17)-1 of the full version of the Model.

5. See, in particular, Recommendation 9 of the Report:

   that countries consider including in their tax conventions provisions aimed at restricting the entitlement to treaty benefits for entities and income covered by measures constituting harmful tax practices and consider how the existing provisions of their tax conventions can be applied for the same purpose; that the Model Tax Convention be modified to include such provisions or clarifications as are needed in that respect.

6. Paragraph 20 of the Commentary on Article 1.

7. Paragraph 21.4 of the Commentary on Article 1.

8. See www.treasury.gov/resource-center/tax-policy/treaties/Documents/Treaty-Limitation-on-Benefits-5-20-2015.pdf

9. The drafting of this Article will depend on how the Contracting States decide to implement their common intention to eliminate double taxation without creating opportunities for non-taxation or reduced taxation through tax evasion or avoidance, including through treaty shopping arrangements. This could be done either through the adoption of paragraph 7 only, through the adoption of the detailed version of paragraphs 1 to 6 that is described in the Commentary on Article [X] together with the implementation of an anti-conduit mechanism as described in paragraph [x] of that Commentary, or through the adoption of paragraph 7 together with any variation of paragraphs 1 to 6 described in the Commentary on Article [X].

10. Paragraphs 1 to 6 and the Commentary thereon are in square brackets pending their finalisation.

11. One assumption that led to the inclusion of paragraph 4 was that Action 5 (Counter harmful tax practices more effectively, taking into account transparency and substance) and Action 8 (Intangibles) of the BEPS Action Plan will address BEPS concerns that may arise from a derivative benefits provision that would apply not only to dividends but also to base-eroding payments such as royalties. The inclusion of paragraph 4 will therefore need to be examined based on the outcome of the work on these Action items and on alternative means of addressing those BEPS concerns such as the measure on "special tax regimes" described in Section C of this Report.

12. Paragraph 16 of that report.

13. Paragraph 23 of the Commentary on Article 4 of the 1963 Draft Convention.

14. See www.treasury.gov/resource-center/tax-policy/treaties/Documents/Treaty-Exempt-Permanent-Establishments-5-20-2015.pdf.

15. Under the principles of public international law, as codified in Articles 26 and 27 of the Vienna Convention on the Law of Treaties (VCLT), if the application of a domestic anti-abuse rule has the effect of allowing a State that is party to a tax treaty to tax an item of income that that State is not allowed to tax under the provisions of the treaty, the application of the domestic anti-abuse rule would conflict with the provisions of the treaty and these treaty provisions should prevail.

16. The saving clause and its exceptions read as follows in the US Model:

    4. Except to the extent provided in paragraph 5, this Convention shall not affect the taxation by a Contracting State of its residents (as determined under Article 4 (Resident)) and its citizens. Notwithstanding the other provisions of this Convention, a former citizen or former long-term resident of a Contracting State may be taxed in accordance with the laws of that Contracting State.

    5. The provisions of paragraph 4 shall not affect:

    a) the benefits conferred by a Contracting State under paragraph 2 of Article 9 (Associated Enterprises), paragraph 7 of Article 13 (Gains), subparagraph b) of paragraph 1, paragraphs 2, 3 and 6 of Article 17 (Pensions, Social Security, Annuities, Alimony, and Child Support), paragraph 3 of Article 18 (Pension Funds), and Articles 23 (Relief From Double Taxation), 24 (Non-Discrimination), and 25 (Mutual Agreement Procedure); and

    b) the benefits conferred by a Contracting State under paragraph 1 of Article 18 (Pension Funds), Articles 19 (Government Service), 20 (Students and Trainees), and 27 (Members of Diplomatic Missions and Consular Posts), upon individuals who are neither citizens of, nor have been admitted for permanent residence in, that State.

17. "2. The context for the purpose of the interpretation of a treaty shall comprise, in addition to the text, including its preamble and annexes:

    (a) Any agreement relating to the treaty which was made between all the parties in connexion with the conclusion of the treaty;

    (b) Any instrument which was made by one or more parties in connexion with the conclusion of the treaty and accepted by the other parties as an instrument related to the treaty."

18. The Commentary on the 1966 Draft of the Vienna Convention on the Law of Treaties notes that the International Court of Justice "has more than once had recourse to the statement of the object and purpose of the treaty in the preamble in order to interpret a particular provision" (Draft Articles on the Law of Treaties with commentaries, Report of the International Law Commission to the General Assembly, Yearbook of the International Law Commission, 1966, vol. II, p. 221).

19. See www.treasury.gov/resource-center/tax-policy/treaties/Documents/Treaty-Special-Tax-Regimes-5-20-2015.pdf and www.treasury.gov/resource-center/tax-policy/treaties/Documents/Treaty-Subsequent-Changes-in-Law-5-20-2015.pdf.

Bibliography

OECD (2015a), *Neutralising the Effects of Hybrid Mismatch Arrangements, Action 2 – 2015 Final Report*, OECD/G20 Base Erosion and Profit Shifting Project, OECD Publishing, Paris, http://dx.doi.org/10.1787/9789264241138-en.

OECD (2015b), *Preventing the Artificial Avoidance of Permanent Establishment Status, Action 7 – 2015 Final Report*, OECD/G20 Base Erosion and Profit Shifting Project, OECD Publishing, Paris, http://dx.doi.org/10.1787/9789264241220-en.

OECD (2014), *Preventing the Granting of Treaty Benefits in Inappropriate Circumstances*, OECD Publishing, Paris, http://dx.doi.org/10.1787/9789264219120-en.

OECD (2013), *Action Plan on Base Erosion and Profit Shifting*, OECD Publishing, Paris, http://dx.doi.org/10.1787/9789264202719-en.

OECD (2012), *Model Tax Convention on Income and on Capital 2010 (Full Version)*, OECD Publishing, Paris, http://dx.doi.org/10.1787/9789264175181-en.

OECD (2010), *The Granting of Treaty Benefits with Respect to the Income of Collective Investment Vehicles*, OECD, Paris, www.oecd.org/ctp/treaties/45359261.pdf.

OECD (2008), *Tax Treaty Issues Related to REITs*, OECD, Paris, www.oecd.org/tax/treaties/39554788.pdf.

OECD (1998), *Harmful Tax Competition: An Emerging Global Issue*, OECD Publishing, Paris, http://dx.doi.org/10.1787/9789264162945-en.

ORGANISATION FOR ECONOMIC CO-OPERATION AND DEVELOPMENT

The OECD is a unique forum where governments work together to address the economic, social and environmental challenges of globalisation. The OECD is also at the forefront of efforts to understand and to help governments respond to new developments and concerns, such as corporate governance, the information economy and the challenges of an ageing population. The Organisation provides a setting where governments can compare policy experiences, seek answers to common problems, identify good practice and work to co-ordinate domestic and international policies.

The OECD member countries are: Australia, Austria, Belgium, Canada, Chile, the Czech Republic, Denmark, Estonia, Finland, France, Germany, Greece, Hungary, Iceland, Ireland, Israel, Italy, Japan, Korea, Luxembourg, Mexico, the Netherlands, New Zealand, Norway, Poland, Portugal, the Slovak Republic, Slovenia, Spain, Sweden, Switzerland, Turkey, the United Kingdom and the United States. The European Union takes part in the work of the OECD.

OECD Publishing disseminates widely the results of the Organisation's statistics gathering and research on economic, social and environmental issues, as well as the conventions, guidelines and standards agreed by its members.

OECD PUBLISHING, 2, rue André-Pascal, 75775 PARIS CEDEX 16
(23 2015 33 1 P) ISBN 978-92-64-24120-6 – 2015

www.ingramcontent.com/pod-product-compliance
Lightning Source LLC
Chambersburg PA
CBHW061222240926
51846CB00006B/1324